DISCOVER PREHISTORIC DARTMOOR

A WALKER'S GUIDE TO THE MOORLAND'S ANCIENT MONUMENTS

WILLIAM D. LETHBRIDGE

HALSGROVE

First published in Great Britain in 2015

Copyright © William D. Lethbridge 2015

British Library Cataloguing-in-Publication Data
A CIP record for this title is available from the British Library

ISBN 978 0 85704 249 1

HALSGROVE
Halsgrove House,
Ryelands Business Park,
Bagley Road, Wellington, Somerset TA21 9PZ
Tel: 01823 653777   Fax: 01823 216796
email: sales@halsgrove.com

Part of the Halsgrove group of companies
Information on all Halsgrove titles is available at: www.halsgrove.com

Printed and bound in China by Everbest Printing Co Ltd

AUTHOR'S INTRODUCTION

Having enjoyed the success of my first publication *One Man's Moor*, I have now completed the present work. I have trekked Dartmoor's wide spaces for just over forty years, studying and photographing everything of interest, including the prehistoric remains of this wonderful landscape.

Over many years, my wife and I have also visited the prehistoric sites in France, witnessing in awe the wonders of Carnac and the tumulus on the island of Gavrinis, the massive dolmen of La Roche aux Fées, the broken menhir at Locmariaquer, and Barnenez where one huge cairn houses eleven chambers. Besides those mentioned we have visited many, many more including the megalithic monuments on the Channel Islands of Guernsey and Jersey.

On our trips to Ireland, especially in County Meath, my wife and I have wondered at the passage tombs of Newgrange, Knowth and Dowth, along with the cemeteries of Loughcrew high up on hills of that same county. But no matter where I have studied these monuments of our past, Dartmoor's fascinating prehistory will always pull me back and intrigue my senses. Why? I think it is because nothing is signposted, it is all out in the wild, to discover for yourself, mostly far from the beaten track. It's often a trek to get there, an adventure, not only just for me, but for those who have ventured out there with me; those who have wanted to see why I spend so much time out there in the midst of the Moor.

Although Dartmoor is full of prehistoric remains there is no doubt that yet more are to be discovered. In fact not long after I completed this work, Alan Endacott discovered a stone circle to the south-west of Sittaford Tor. He, like myself and many others, has trekked Dartmoor for years and, as with all explorers, lived in hope of making a find like this. First he noticed a couple of flat rectangular boulders lying a couple of yards apart, then with a search found more forming a semi circle, while suspecting there would be others buried beneath the moorland surface to complete a full circle. Since then Jane Marchand, Phil Newman and volunteers from the Dartmoor Preservation Association have been involved, verifying that what Mr Endacott had discovered was the real thing, a prehistoric stone circle.

William D. Lethbridge
Plympton 2014

DEDICATION

I dedicate this work to my wife, Sandy
and my late good friend, Garth.

ACKNOWLEDGEMENTS

My thanks go to those who have put up with my sometimes over-zealous endeavours to complete this work, especially my wife Sandy who has accompanied me over the miles and years on my sometimes strenuous field work. Thanks also go to Bob Williams and Garth Morrison for their occasional excursions with me, especially for holding the other end of my tape measure. Special thanks goes to "Paisley" my Jack Russell my friend, my mate, my constant moorland companion who is with me every stride of the way and more.

I would also like to acknowledge the works of William Crossing, R.H. Worth, Samuel Rowe, John L.W. Page and Mr Robert Burnard.

Thanks also go to my two sons-in-law John Thompson and Simon Mathews for all the help they have given me when my computer skills have frustratingly let me down.

*It trickles from the moor through the peat, from a moss-covered swelling on a hill.
From near the brow or halfway down, it trickles quietly under the sunlight
and clouds and mist; the whisper of a breeze, the rustling of the wind. It trickles while the
bracken sways and the heather flowers, and where the occasional heath-spotted orchids grow.
Where the raven can be heard, along with the pipit and the skylark, beneath where flocks of
curlew dance their aerobatics in the sky; where the cuckoo can be heard when it first arrives
in spring. It gathers pace where rivulets emerge into its run and widens, till the sound of its
rushing comes splashing gurgling and bubbling over pebbles and boulders till a cataract
cascades into a crystal clear pool. Except for the ruins of the Bronze Age, not a
dwelling can be seen. Not a tarmac road or its vehicles heard.
Tranquility.* – William D. Lethbridge

For those unfamiliar with the landscape of Dartmoor and the principal types of prehistoric remains included in this book, the following descriptions may be helpful.

CAIRNS

Cairns, also referred to as barrows, are mounds of stones, all varying in size from about 10' to well over 100', some covering a cist, others covering multiple interments. Some of these features have a ring of set stones surrounding them to hold the mound in place. Also to be found are ring cairns, small circles of stones set in the ground, examples of which can be found on Ringmoor Down, in the Drizzlecombe Valley. A few stones of such a specimen can be located above Cholwich Town Waste to the east of the huge cairn, and two are situated high up on Cosdon Hill.

CISTS (KISTVAEN)

A cist is a stone coffin (sarcophagus) comprising two side stones, two end stones and a lid. The side and end stones are normally flat slabs of granite, whereas the lid can be of any shape, as long as its underside fits comfortably on the top. Langcombe Brook cist (shown here) which measures 39" by 23" provides a good example regarding average size. The deceased was generally interred in a crouched position. Ashes of cremated remains have been found in urns tucked into one corner of the cist; no significant human remains have been found in any cist on Dartmoor owing to the acidity of the soil.

CROMLECHS (DOLMEN)

The only surviving specimen within the confines of the Dartmoor National Park is near Drewsteignton. This a restoration of 1862. However other ruins that can be seen on Dartmoor, are on Cuckoo Ball and on Corringdon Ball. The last mentioned feature still displays a good 43-yard length of its collapsed and ruined barrow. Another possible example is the feature associated with the rock piles of Hawks Tor on the south-west slopes of Shaugh Moor.

HUT CIRCLES (ROUND HOUSES)

Only the low granite walls survive of these features. Many of those that were built for human habitation still have their door jambs in place, often remaining in their upright position after standing for as long as four thousand years. Hut circles vary in size with a diameters from 6' up to 30'. There are well over three thousand of them to be found on the moor. The hut circle shown here has no obvious doorway and was possibly used for some other purpose than human occupation.

MENHIRS

The name menhir comes from the Breton language and describes a tall stone. On Dartmoor these great monoliths are often associated with other prehistoric sites, such as stone rows. It can be reasonably surmised they were erected to fulfil a ceremonial function associated with religious rites, or the marking of seasonal changes. However, some of these stones can be found in isolation, such as the stone named Beardown Man high up on the moor near Devil's Tor. This magnificent specimen, shown in the photograph here, is 14' in height, the tallest on the moor.

REAVES

These features are prehistoric land divisions, thought to date from the early Bronze Age period, separating one territorial boundary from another, a bit like the parishes we have today. They are generally constructed by throwing up stones and soil forming walls that in some cases run for a few miles such as the one that crosses Walkhampton

Common. Others subdivide land into field systems, such as the classic examples on Holne Moor and at Vag Hill, both situated above the river Dart.

STONE CIRCLES

There are twelve known true stone circles on Dartmoor, with stones varying in height from barely showing above the ground to just over 7' 5" high. Nearly all, except for one, has seen the hand of modern man helping in their restoration. The specimen that hasn't been restored lies above the Teign at Scorhill but this has been much disfigured by man who has removed seven of the circle's members for use elsewhere; all seven are written about within the pages of this book.

STONE ROWS

There is estimated to be over seventy stone rows on Dartmoor. These wonderful structures are thought to be ceremonial avenues. All vary in their make up, obviously designed by their individual architects for reasons of their own liking, and include single rows, double rows and triple rows of aligned stones. Some rows have a menhir at one end. Others are designed with a blocking stone at one end like the double row at Hurston Ridge shown in the photograph here, which as one can see also displays a menhir and the remains of a cairn. Some have a plain cairn at one end, others boast more a lavish cairn circle or, as on Shovel Down, a double row displaying a triple circle of stones fronting it.

None of us knows what life was like in prehistoric times, we can only guess. Most of what we say about what remains can be found on the rugged terrain of the moor is merely conjecture. No one knows exactly when the beautiful but crude granite structures were erected, no one knows why the peoples of their day chose to place them where they did, where we find them to gaze in awe and wonder at today. Not even those who distinguish themselves with a doctorate in archaeology to their name – the experts in their field – they too, like the layman, can only presume.

The science of carbon dating can take us a fair way into determining when an item was placed where we find it today, but even with this technology it is still only an estimate.

The function of the cist of course is self explanatory, it is what we are looking at, a stone coffin. We look at a stone row, however, and as individuals we see what we want to perceive it to be. Is it a ceremonial avenue where the deceased was carried by pallbearers to his or her last resting place in the grave beneath the cairn at the end of the row? But then not every stone alignment has a cairn situated at its end. Or were such monuments erected in honour of the deceased, a kind of exaggerated headstone? It could well be all of these things, along with their possible use to predict and record astronomical alignments – employed to forecast the winter and summer solstices, or determining certain important times of the year – a calendar if you like. It is thought by some that the stone circles were built for meeting and trading places, if this was so what was the purpose of the two circles only a few feet apart, known as the Grey Wethers on the slopes of Sittaford Tor? Some people see the circles as places for worship, other see them as theatres for rituals, perhaps offering some poor soul's life to the gods.

In this book I concentrate mainly on the cist (kistvaen), stone rows and stone circles. However, it doesn't mean that the existence of the cairns, hut circles, enclosures and field systems are any less important. Nor am I going to pretend that I know all there is to know about what I come across. Most, in fact nearly all the knowledge I possess, I have learned from Dartmoor explorers past and present. However in saying that, I have in my nearly forty years of trekking across the moor's wonderful landscape discovered a few items of interest previously unknown to the record books.

My interest in all there is to see began by coming across a bracken-shrouded circle of stones on Shaugh Moor, just above the china clay works where I was employed. The circle, complete with an entrance, was set within a much larger tumbled walled area. The complex intrigued me and I enquired from colleagues who lived locally what it was. "Tham were the houses of the old people that live up yer years and years ago. What you'm seen is only what's left of 'um, you'll find loads of 'um further out on the moor." Their response aroused my curiosity even further and eventually led me to visit libraries and the local interest shelves in bookshops.

Robert Burnard's photograph of fellow members of the Dartmoor Exploration Committee at Headland Warren stone row, August 1893.

Doe Tor cist

It turned out that the circle of tumbled stones was a hut circle and before long I was into Crossing and Worth and delving into other works, most of which I now have stacked on my own bookshelves. Since the time of Mr Crossing and Mr Worth many more relics of the past have been discovered, just as there will be more found after my days of walking the moor are over.

*   *   *

Most Dartmoor monuments lie in areas where rainfall runs into certain rivers, and in order to make this book easier to follow I employ these watersheds and describe those monuments that can be visited within them. Beginning with the rivers that flow to the south, the River Lyd is where our journey starts (please note, the sketch maps employed in this project are included as only a guide and should not be looked upon as accurate).

Doe Tor cist lies in a valley, overlooked by the rock pile that gives it its name, and the twin peaks of Sharp Tor and Hare Tor. Only one side and two end stones remain of the cist, however, there is a stone partly buried a few feet to the east of it that could well be its cap stone. Only three stones of its cairn now show through the turf. To give some idea of the cist's size the one side stone is 50″ long, while the end stones measure 23″ and 30″ respectively. Its lie is 61°N.

Doe Tor cist seen from above.

This could well be the cap stone of Doe Tor cist.

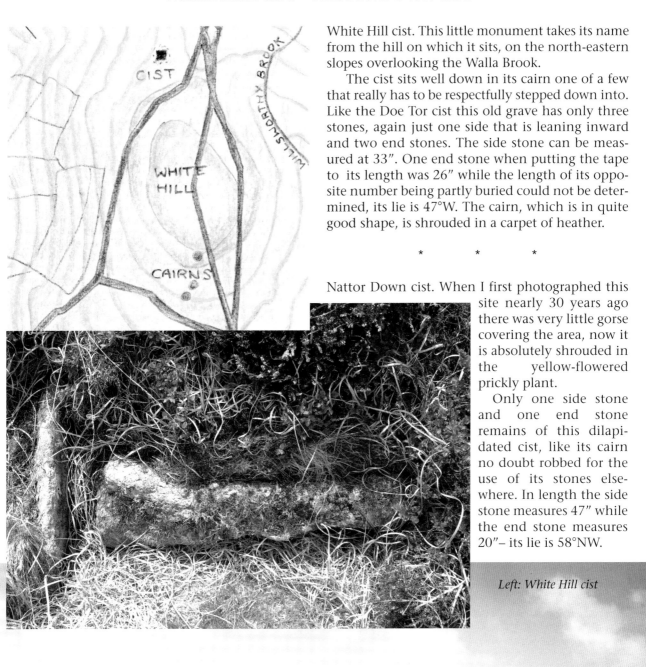

White Hill cist. This little monument takes its name from the hill on which it sits, on the north-eastern slopes overlooking the Walla Brook.

The cist sits well down in its cairn one of a few that really has to be respectfully stepped down into. Like the Doe Tor cist this old grave has only three stones, again just one side that is leaning inward and two end stones. The side stone can be measured at 33". One end stone when putting the tape to its length was 26" while the length of its opposite number being partly buried could not be determined, its lie is 47°W. The cairn, which is in quite good shape, is shrouded in a carpet of heather.

*   *   *

Nattor Down cist. When I first photographed this site nearly 30 years ago there was very little gorse covering the area, now it is absolutely shrouded in the yellow-flowered prickly plant.

Only one side stone and one end stone remains of this dilapidated cist, like its cairn no doubt robbed for the use of its stones elsewhere. In length the side stone measures 47" while the end stone measures 20"– its lie is 58°NW.

Left: White Hill cist

White Hill cairn

11

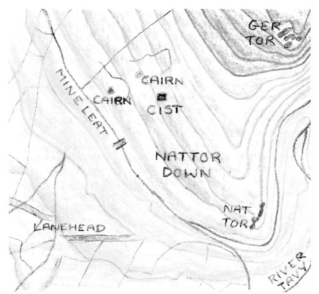

at when one knows that the grave may have been covered with its cairn. To remove a few hundred-weight of stone or soil would not be to much of a chore for someone who cherished the deceased. Its inner length is 53", one end stone is 29" the other 27". Its lie is 59°NNW.

Looking more or less to the east from the cist, the standing stone will be seen. I think its curious shape makes it for me one of the most attractive menhirs on the moor. The picture opposite displays the bullet marks at their best, shot at by troops on manoeuvres during the Second World War. Reading Mr Worth's *Dartmoor* it tells us that prior to 1893 the monument lay on the ground, and its length was 11' 8" now erected it stands 9' 2". Another un-usual thing about the stone is that unlike all the other standing stones on the moor, it is not granite. It stands at the south end of a single stone row, and

The Tavy Watershed not only the holds the Nattor Down cist, but also in its fold is a cist, a stone row and a fascinating standing stone (menhir.) The cist lies only a few yards from three grass-covered cairns. The cist lies on the gentle eastern slopes of White Tor where an Iron Age fort can be found sur-rounding the great eminence. The White Tor cist like the three that I have already described, has the side stone missing, but why this should be I doubt if anyone knows. It as been surmised by one com-mentator that it may have never been put in place, left out of its structure for the purpose of placing certain offerings inside. A theory not to be sniffed

The view over the Langstone Moor cist

Above: Langstone Moor cist

Left: Langstone Moor menhir

Langstone Moor stone row

in the Lake District. Most of the stones of its circumference now lie in ruins, blown to pieces by the same disrespectful persons that tried to blast the menhir into fragments. All the stones lay prostrate during Samuel Rowe's visit. About a year after the menhir had been re-erected it fell over. The stones of the circle were re-erected and in the watercolour below, painted by the artist F. J. Widgery, there appear to be fifteen stones standing, with one outlier situated a couple of yards away from the main stones of the circle. Now only nine stones stand in their place on the hillside.

Above: F. J. Widgery's painting 'Sacred Circle, Langstone Moor', dated from c.1895 showing at least fifteen uprights in place.

Below: Resulting from the circle being used for target practice by the military in World War Two, only a few stones remain in place today.

at the end of the alignment's northern extremity one can see what appears to be the remains of a cairn. The stones of the row are small and now few and far between, eighteen just poked their peeks above the turf in Worth's day. Now, with a keen eye, only a dozen can be seen. In the photo above the menhir is in view.

We are now sitting on the Walkham watershed where the stone circle on Langstone Moor must have surely been almost equal in terms of its setting on the moor and the panorama to be enjoyed from it, to the magnificent monument of Castlerigg situated high on the hills above the town of Keswick

Main picture: Barn Hill cist

Inset: The cist in situ

This little grave (above) is situated on the slopes of Barn Hill. Both side stones and the two end stones are still in place after surviving the elements thrown at them over the three to four thousand years of the cist's existence. The only blot on its presence is the lack of its cap stone. There appears to be very little of the cairn that may have once covered it. In saying that, the author Laurence Flanagan, archaeologist and author of *A Dictionary of Irish Archaeology*, suggest that some cists may not necessarily have been covered with a cairn.

Walkers stroll down the track past this little grave on the way to the ancient cross of Windy Post and may not know it is there. Although the photograph above doesn't reveal it, the area behind the photographer is littered with boulders of various proportions, and perhaps that is why the grave was not

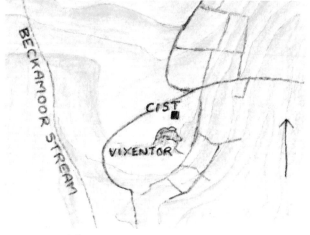

mentioned by Crossing and Worth, nor Samuel Rowe. They too may have trekked passed it on their way to Windy Post, not realising it was there.

One side stone of the cist is leaning inwards and one end stone is leaning out, both interior sides measure the same 41" while the width is 27" tapering to 22". Its lie is North.

Vixen Tor cist is situated inside land that is now off limits to the public since the landowner fenced it and put it out of bounds. By the time it came around for me to think of recording its dimensions and its lie, it was to late, the gate to the property was closed and locked. The cist is complete, with one end consisting of two stones, the two slabs leaning against it, is the dislodged cap stone.

Vixen Tor cist

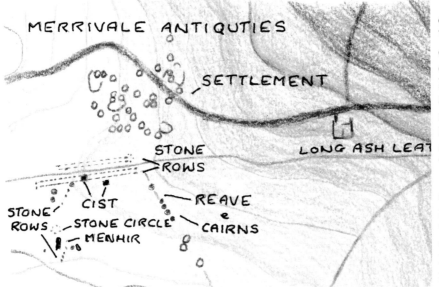

To the east, high up on the other side of the River Walkham lies one of the most complete prehistoric landscapes on Dartmoor, known as the Merrivale complex. Here there are stone rows, a stone circle, a menhir, two cists, cairns and hut circles. The whole site lies only a few yards from the main Tavistock/Princetown road.

The photograph inset below shows the first of the stone rows, Row A, for visitors to wonder at as they approach the complex from the car parks that lie beside the main road. There is a remnant of a cairn circle adjoining the so-called blocking stone that stands looking along the length of the alignment. The character of the avenue has over the years been despoiled with several of it members removed for one reason or another. According to Worth's *Dartmoor*, this row measures 198 yards and a few feet. Walking its length one can see that its stones appear to diminish in height and proportion as our footsteps lead us toward its sad-looking west end.

Its neighbour, Row B, below, displays a much more uniform appearance with every stone standing well above the turf. Its length being 288 yards, it is considerably longer than our first row. Here, more or less in its centre, lies a cist surrounded by a cairn. The lie of the little grave is 1°NNE.

The alignment terminates with two stones that stand higher than any in the row and which were lying on the turf in the days when Samuel Rowe, the man who wrote *A Perambulation of Dartmoor*, walked the Moor.

Merrivale Row A

Merrivale Row B

Merrivale cairn and cist

End of Row B

Merrivale circle

There are two more rows within the complex, both are in a sorry state of preservation compared to Rows A and B. The first, Row C, a single row, runs from a cairn a few yards west from the cisted cairn. It is orientated south-west with a dozen stones barely showing above the ground. Row D can be found to the south of the site's standing stone where only five stones have survived the test of time.

Merrivale menhir

The menhir, or standing stone, as some call it, can be seen to the south of Row B. According to Worth, it stands 10' 4" in height. However, a more recent commentator has it at just under 10 feet. There is a stone just over seven feet long, lying on the ground a few yards to the south-east of the menhir; this specimen apparently once stood upright in the hole beside it.

The stone circle, the smallest on the moor at 62 feet in diameter, rather lets the rest of the Merrivale antiquities down, with only eleven stones now to be counted. And there is very little sign that those visible ever had others to increase their number. No other circle on Dartmoor has so few members, and even those that stand above the turf cannot boast of any significant height.

Not more than a few yards from the cairn and cist, in the centre of stone Row B, can be seen a large cist. To the uninitiated, at first sight, the huge cap stone appears to be nothing more than two large pieces of granite. However, on closer inspection they will notice that the pit below it is lined with flat elongated slabs, making it a stone sarcophagus. One of the largest on the moor, its internal dimensions are 6' 8" long on one side and 6' 5" on the other; its width is 36" at one end, tapering to 31 inches at the other. Its depth is 30 inches. Its direction is 59NNW.

Merrivale cist cap stone

hut circle Merrivale

Plan of the Merrivale Antiquities produced by John Page in 1889.

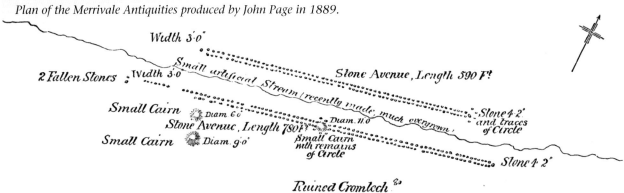

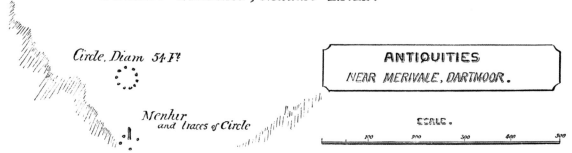

To complete this prehistoric landscape there are forty-one hut circles to be found, most lying to the north-east of the complex, with a few set within enclosures. While enjoying the stroll around these features, the walker will come across comparatively modern mill stone, abandoned years ago for some unknown reason. Some early antiquarians thought this large neatly-carved stone was the cap stone of a dolmen.

* * *

About half a mile to the south-east from the end of the Merrivale southern row, across the Long Ash Brook, the walker arrives at a dilapidated cairn and cist, both sitting on the slopes beneath the grounds of Yellowmead Farm.

 Like many on the moor, just two stones remain of this cist a side stone and a end stone, and to the uninitiated the pair would be passed by without a second glance. The lie of the cist is 7°NE.

Location of the cist near Yellowmeade. Inset: the two stones sitting in the cairn.

18

Ingra Tor cist

Stone row and cist at Horseyeat Farm

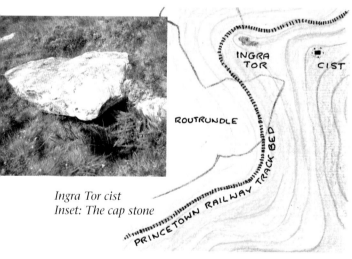

Ingra Tor cist
Inset: The cap stone

On the vast expanse of Walkhampton Common, on the lower WNW slopes of Leeden Tor just above a now dry leat that once ran its water to Routrundle Farm, can be found the so called Ingra Tor cist. This stone grave again has one end stone missing, however, unlike those described so far, this one has its cap stone lying above its bracken-shrouded hollow. To give some idea of its size the side stones measure 59" and 64" respectively, its width is 31" tapering to 28". Its lie is North. The whole sits in a considerable amount of an untidy grass covered cairn.

On the south-west slopes of Walkhampton Common overlooking the outer fields of Horseyeat Farm, is a stone row, apparently unknown to Mr Worth and those antiquarians of note who trekked the moor before him. It was not until the early 1960s that there is any mention of it within the circles of Dartmoor enthusiasts. In the days when this monument was erected, the Black Brook could not have been in existence, for now the infant water of the stream flows through the lower end of the row. Surely those early people would not have placed

Stone row at Horseyeat Farm
Inset: The stone in the brook

The paired stones at Horseyeat Farm

the monument in a watercourse? This row starts uphill from a bracken-covered cairn and ends at a beautiful salmon-pink stone standing (give or take an inch) four foot-three inches high. Where the stream runs through the row the water has eroded its line to the extent of fifty-five feet five inches, whilst doing so it as taken out what can be reasoned to be nine of its members. All nine are now most likely beneath the water and muddy surroundings. However, one has resisted the meandering flow and still stands proudly upright twenty-one feet from the end stone.

An unusual feature of this row is the introduction of double pair halfway down its length. Why,

only those that constructed the monument could have told us. There are two prostrate stones belonging to this row that intrigues, both, apart from the end stone, would have stood considerably taller than their companions; the one nearest the cairn measuring four foot six inches long, the other nearer the end stone is four foot two inches. This feature, if it was standing, is reminiscent of those taller stones in Row B at Merrivale.

*   *   *

The Sharpitor/Stanlake prehistoric complex sits beside the Yelverton to Princetown road. It consists of stone rows, cists, cairns and reaves (boundary works). No striking feature hits the eye on first arriving at Goad Stone Pond, then one or two small stones may be noticed protruding a few inches from the sheep- and pony-nibbled grass. These are members of a double stone row.

Since photographing the row close by Goad Stone Pond in the 1970s, I find that a stone has been removed from the southern alignment, the second stone along the row in the inset photograph on the opposite page.

This row enjoys uniqueness in that it is one of only two on the moor that spreads its stones into two different watersheds, with its cairn in the Walkham and its blocking stone in the Meavy.

Double stone row at Sharpitor
Inset: Photo revealing the second stone
along is now missing

Top: The blocking stone
Above: The single stone row

The stones, where they are to be seen, run in lines to the west towards the dilapidated cairn. The other way, to the east, they run to the two tallest stones of the row and their blocking stone – all three of which were standing upright in Worth's day, for when measuring them he describes them as being standing not prostrate. Yet, William Crossing and the Reverend Rowe appear to suggest the row terminated at the cairn and cist a couple of dozen yards farther down the hill, indicating that the stones were prostrate at the time they were exploring the moor. Now the blocking stone, having toppled forward towards its row, lies on the turf. It measures 3' 6" x 5'. Its two companions, one still standing the other almost prostrate, measure 1' 5" and 3' 8" respectively.

Also to be found here is the blocking stone, which can be seen in the middle photograph, left. In the lower photo to the left is a single stone row. This row is in a very poor state of preservation, no doubt robbed like the double row to aid the laying of the Princetown/Yelverton road just a few yards away to the north. If time is in the modern explorers favour, the stones of what remains of the row can be located. Mr Worth came across only three but close examination reveals up to seven stones for sure. Some have fallen, others merely peek above the turf. If one wants to explore further, examine an imaginary line farther west where one can envisage nearer to twenty stones.

The cairn and cist refered to earlier can be seen in the photographs overleaf. They lie just a stone's throw from the Princetown Road and no doubt

Cairn above the Princetown/Yelverton Road
Inset: The cist

Remains of the double stone row

One of four ruined cairns

robbed of its beauty by those that constructed the highway. Now there is no sign of a cap stone and only four or five stones of the retaining circle remain in place. Like many other cists, one end stone is missing. Another feature of the grave is that one side of it is made up of two stones, the grave is 29″ wide, but owing to the side stone being partially buried the length can not be properly ascertained. It lies 63°N.

Farther down the hill from the cairn and cist, to the north-east the walker will find the remains of a double stone row. The pairs are unusual in that they are set only inches apart, very much like the single pair set in the Horseyeat Row. Only three of the pairs and two or three single stones have survived since they were first placed here. The rest, who

knows where they may have gone; perhaps robbed for road building like that of the other three monuments, or even utilised by the constructers of the reave that runs down the hill from Sharpitor before making its way along the great stretch of Walkhampton Common. The stone row starts from the sad remains of a cairn and descends the hill until nearly reaching the reave, after which there seems to be no evidence at all that it ever existed beyond the old land division.

Beyond the reave four cairns can be found, all with far more of their bulk remaining than the mound related to the double row. All four have at some time been delved into by the curious. However, only one of the mounds ever contained a cist. This cairn like the others as been disturbed, gouged through, leaving some remains piled to one side. No cap stone can now be found and one end stone is missing. To give some idea of its size the two side stones measure 48″ and 50″, its width is 31″ tapering to 29″. Its lie is 61°N. What survives of the cairns retaining circle lay in disarray on the turf.

* * *

Leather Tor cist can be found to the left of the Leather Tor Farm track. The cist sits in the considerable mound of its cairn; the mound also retains a few stones of its retaining circle. The cist is complete, except the cap stone is missing and the southern end stone as been moved a few feet away, next to where the cap stone is thought to be half buried. The size of the grave can be imagined when measuring the side stones at 59″ and 64″, its width at 31″ tapering to 28″. Its lie is 63°N.

* * *

Leeden Tor stone row (see over) is not very photogenic, the stones being few and far between, plus the fact that the hillside is shrouded in long grass and gorse, which doesn't inspire a scene of much interesting spectacle. The stones run down the hill from a much dilapidated cairn that intermingles with a reave which also runs down the hill from the rock piles of Leeden Tor above which gives the row its name.

Determining the amount of stones there are in the row, one can count at fifteen in all. Some are standing, others lie on the turf, the longest of those when the tape measure is placed over it, measures five feet. It would surely, if it were standing, have been the tallest of those to be seen now in the row.

The reave that runs through the short double stone row on the north-eastern slope of Sharpitor, also runs through this row and, thus, two reaves in-

Leather Tor cist

Inset: The cist

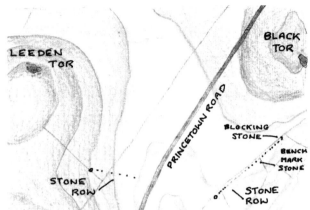

Stanlake double stone row

Leeden Tor stone row

Stanlake - the blocking stone

The Stanlake double stone row runs along the north-western perimeter newtake hedge of Stanlake Farm. It is a shame that the hedge builders felt it necessary to bury one of the alignments. However, it is possible to spot the occasional hint of a lost stone or two in the outside walling as one walks along it. The row starts on its run south-west from a cairn, much dilapidated, with the hints of two other cairns close by. Like the longer of the two Sharpitor Rows, this one climbs a slight incline for the first few yards before the ground levels out, after which it runs along to a huge blocking stone half buried in the hedge. There is in the row one stone with a bench mark etched on its top right hand corner.

terfering with the row's alignment may well be the reason for its poor condition. Some examples of spacing between the stones is, 31' 4", 41' 8", 21' 8" and 23' and 25'.

*　　　*　　　*

*　　　*　　　*

Hart Tor double stone row

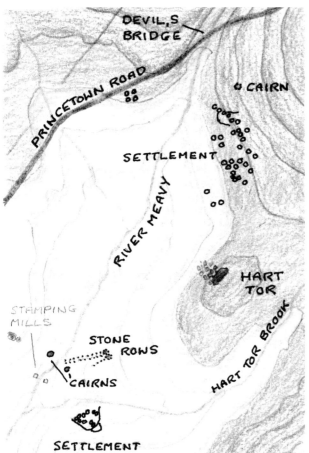

A view across Hart Tor stone row

robbed and has a tinners' gully running through it, is the more complete. The bottom end of it has been obliterated by the tinners who worked over this part of the River Meavy. Its cairn has stood the test of time, with its circumference still contained well with the retaining stones, where most of them remain standing.

The single row has suffered far more from what's been thrown at it over the centuries. Only seventeen stones can now be recognised and its terminus cannot be found. Like the double row, the same tinners' gully runs through it. Although its cairn sits beside the double rows, its aspect is nowhere near as spectacular.

The two alignments at Hart Tor consist of a double and a single row. They both run from their respective cairns. The double row although it as been

RADDICK HILL CAIRN AND CIST

Part of Hart Tor single stone row and its cairn

Raddick Hill cairn

Inset: The ruined cist

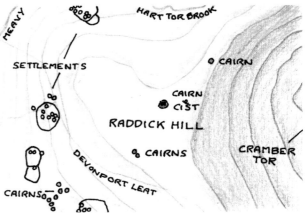

Raddick Hill cairn and cist lie upon the slopes of Raddick Hill where can be found four enclosures. Inside the enclosure above the Hart Tor Brook, while excavating within a hut circle in 1896, Robert Barnard discovered a cooking pot. It measured ten and half inches in height and ten inches in diameter. The artefact had apparently survived the years since the hut's abandonment as a result of a section of the inner wall that had fallen inward and covered the cooking hole. However, when an attempt to was made to raise the treasured item, further digging had to be done, and in its fragile condition it broke leaving an inch or two of its bottom behind in the soil. The pot was eventually successfully raised and displayed in Plymouth City Museum.

Along with the huts and enclosures, thirteen cairns can be found, eight of them together in a group, cemetery-like. None however contain a cist; it is only the largest of those on the hillside that holds a stone chamber within its fold. This, like the monument on White Hill in the Lyd catchment area, involves stepping down into the cairn to examine the cist. It measures 47" long by 29" wide by 13" deep. With part of the cist still covered, it appears that it may have been capped with more than one stone. The lie of the cist is 52°WNW. Since taking my photograph someone has exposed the cist a little more by displacing some of the stones.

*   *   *

DOWN TOR CAIRN AND CISTS

Down in the valley of the Newleycombe Lake are three cist's grouped together like a small family cemetery. It reminded my grandson of the story of the three bears for there is a large cist, a medium cist and a small one. If approaching from the beautiful Newleycombe Lake, the group can be located north-east of Down Tor, just forty-five walking paces up hill from a massive granite boulder. It is interesting to try and speculate where the folk who were interred here, once resided. The answer could have been the group of hut circles to the north of Down Tor, for the graves almost share the same contours as the old circular ruins.

There is a leat running through the little cemetery, cut by the tinners, respectfully I think, only the flowing water over time eroding the southern edge of cairn No.3. All four stones of cist No.1 are still in place. The only thing that mars its appearance is the missing cap stone. To give some idea of the size of the grave compared to the other two, the length is 52" and 29" in width at one end tapering

A hut circle, Down Tor

to 22" at the other. Its depth at this time is 18". Its lie is North. Cist No.2 has a length of 40", one side stone is leaning outwards to one side. If in place the whole would have had the same appearance as cost

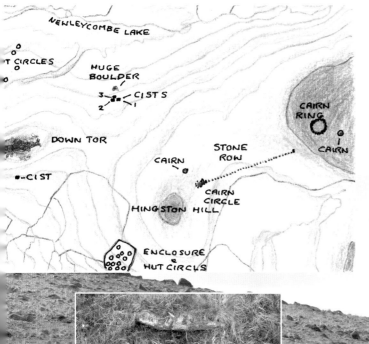

Main photo: The author at Down Tor cairn

Inset above left and right: cist No.1 and cist No.2, below cist No.3

Left: The southern slopes of Down Tor

Inset: The cist

No.1, in that it would be seen to be tapering, for the end stones differ in length with one being 26" while the other is only 19", its depth is like No.1 is 18". The cap stone could well be the partially buried slab to the east, near the edge of the grave. Its lie is again North. Cist No.3, across the old disused leat, the smallest of the three, measures just 12" in width. Its original length cannot be precisely ascertained, but, to give some idea of its length, the two side stones are a mere 17" long. The cap stone is nowhere to be seen. Its lie is 54°WNW. The distance between No.1 and No.2 is 35' 8", between No.2 and No.3 it is 12' 6", and between No.3 and No.1 it is 35' 3".

On the Southern slopes of Down Tor, if a search is made, can be found another cist. Its cairn is camouflaged in the steep slope of the hill, but it is there and reveals itself clearly once located. The one end stone that remains in place, is situated between the two side stones, but its opposite number is missing,

and consequently the length of the cist cannot be ascertained for certain. However if the stone was in place and positioned so as it met the ends of both the side stones, its inner length would measure 51" and 49" respectively. The width, although it doesn't appear to be so, is 26" at one end, and 25" at the other. Its lie is 48°W. The cap stone lies downhill on the side of the cairn.

*   *   *

The prize monument in this area lies more or less to the east, up on Hingston Hill. Although there are other wonderful sites to experience on the moor, Hingston offers, in my opinion, the most magnificent of all prehistoric monuments on Dartmoor.

However all is not what it seems, for this beautiful specimen of a monument, although prehistoric in age, has been restored; that is to say the menhirs and a great deal of the cairn circle after being found

Hingston Hill stone circle and stone row

fallen and badly disturbed were fondly placed back in their socket holes in 1894 under the guidance of Robert Burnard, the Rev W.A.G. Grey and S. Baring-Gould, with the spade work carried out by Messrs Turpin of Plymouth. But, nothing can be taken away from the spectacle when one climbs the hill and the monument comes into view.

The Circle is made up of twenty-five stones, except for one or two they are nearly all of fairly substantial size, with the tallest being nearly four feet in height. From the circle the row runs along to the east-north-east, starting at a nine-foot-six-inch tall menhir and after travelling 381 yards along one hundred and sixty one stones, it terminates at a five-foot high blocking stone standing at right angles to the alignment.

This most impressive feature, known as Down Tor stone row, should come under the name of the hill it sits on, Hingston Hill. Looking back along the row from the blocking stone, as one can see the photograph above right, the row is not straight; it veers a little to the east as the blocking stone is approached from the circle.

The row is not orientated towards the centre of an enclosure that lies to the north-east of the row's blocking stone as one commentator suggests. In fact, if it were to have continued its length farther, it would have just missed the southern side of a considerably large cairn that sits to the east-south-east of the enclosure. An interesting feature of this

beautiful stone row, is that it dips near the middle of its run but still maintains more or less the same height at both ends.

*   *   *

Other than some boundary works and a cist, the higher portions of Leeden Hill are somewhat devoid of prehistoric remains, that is until its lower slopes are reached where the hillside begins to converge with Yellowmead Down. Here can be found another cist, a stone row (with a question mark against it), a couple of cairns and a beautiful four-fold stone circle. There are also seven other mounds of possible cairns.

The Rev Sabine Baring Gould overseeing work on the 1894 restoration

Above: Hingston Hill stone row leading up to the cairn Circle.

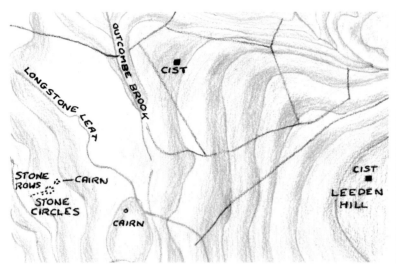

The three boulders above Deancombe Brook

Leeden Hill cist

Below: Remains of the cist

A feature that should not be missed whilst out in the area is to be found in the steep sloping fields above the south bank of the Deancombe Brook. Three boulders of obviously different proportions stand not quite in line, running more or less in a north-south direction down the hill. The distance between them is 35' 6" and 45'. Their heights are 27", 36" and 68" respectively as one walks down across the field. However, these stones in my opinion, deserve a closer look.

The Outcombe cist is so called because it is situated high above the old ruined farmstead of that name. It sits in what can now be seen of the scant remains of its cairn, surrounded by the many pits dug into the moor by the tinners. As the photo below shows, only three stones remain in situ. To give some idea of the size of the cist, the internal length of the one side stone is 32", its opposite number must have protruded beyond the 25" smaller end stone and met the longer 33" end stone nigh on mid-way along its length. The cist's lie is 3°NNE 35°SSW.

Leeden Hill cist sits near the crest of the hill in a little oasis of green, overlooking spectacular views as far as the magnificent Walkham Tors and the Cornish moors. The cist, or the remains if it, lie in a sorry state in the slight pit of its cairn with only one end stone visible and two stones that make up one side. The cap stone leans against a jumble of stones that cannot be described as anything but that, that is until an excavation can determine its value to the dilapidated feature. To give some idea of the cist's size, the length of the one side is, 52" while the width is 31". Its lie is 53°WNW 21°SSW.

Two set stones on the north-west edge of the cairn could be what remains of a retaining circle.

The Outcombe cist

Inset: Remains of the cist

Yellowmead Fourfold stone circle is a wonderful monument to view. A reconstruction, I know, it is nevertheless a magical piece of prehistoric 'art'. Like the Hingston Hill stone row we have to thank the enthusiastic antiquarians of the past for this restoration. Although it wasn't Mr Worth who re-erected the stones, he was however the first to identify them, clothed in a coating of moorland vegetation. The ninety-nine stone monument owes its present day appearance to a team that worked along with the Rev. Hugh Breton. Although some of the stones were sadly missing and couldn't be replaced, it is still a striking monument, especially when the grass in winter has turned golden and the sun is shining across it from low in the sky.

The diameter of the monument from east to west is approximately 61' 6". North to south it is 65'. The stones of the inner circle are set considerably closer than those of the other three, no doubt employed to hold the mound that covered an interment in place. There is a suspicion, that the spectacle we see today, is only a part of what was first constructed by the people of prehistory, for here to be seen are other stones, forming stone rows, including two that run beyond an old disused leat. Other stones that stand at right angles to the outer circle are evidence of the outset of five more rows, perhaps robbed of their true lengths, like the missing stones of the circles, for the building of the Yellowmead Farm boundary stone walling, that stands down hill, just a few yards away.

When Mr Worth drew his plan of the circles there were one hundred and four stones in situ; he also placed six stones at right angles to the circles, while the double row contained eight members. However his plan did not show any stones on the far side of the old disused leat.

Today only six stones survive in the double row, only five stand at right angles, and I can count one

hundred and six stones that make up the circles. numbering 24, 27, 32 and 23 respectively. Who knows, perhaps the monument was never completed and we today are looking at what was finished, remaining for us to ponder over.

Although not in such a good state of preservation, a smaller cairn circle with only three stones of its retaining circle remaining in situ, can be seen a little farther up the slope of the hill to the east.

To the south-east of the cairn circles, a truly fascinating cluster of earth and stone mounds can be located, situated just a little over a hundred yards from some old tin streaming that descends down the hillside. There are seven mounds in all and as far as I know, all the writers of Dartmoor's antiquities have either ignored them, dismissing them as nothing of archaeological importance or were merely unaware of their presence. However, as a

Yellowmead Fourfold stone circle

Inset (top): Two rows running away from the circle and (below) four stones at right angles to the circle

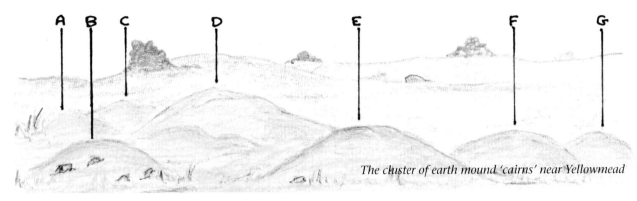

A B C D E F G

The cluster of earth mound 'cairns' near Yellowmead

The seven earth mound 'cairns'

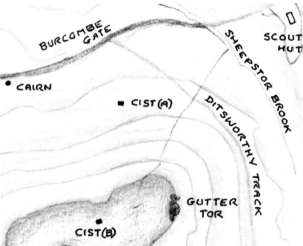

Gutter Tor cist

layman, I will leave it to the archaeologist to determine their reasons for being there. I personally do not think the mounds are the work of the tinners, nor the result of stone clearing the nearby acreage, for why place them where they are, covering a good yardage of feeding ground, when they could have been heaped into the corner of the nearby boundary wall. The mounds all vary in height and diameter and a couple have had their centres thrown out, one in particular as been so distorted that in now appears to be oblong in shape. However, here I may be misguided and the oblong shape may be the distortion of two cairns joined together by the throwing out of both. The drawing above that I have produced for this record is not to scale, the cairns, especially E, F and G belong a little further to the right. They all vary in size, cairn (A), the smallest, has a diameter of 8' 8", (B) is 12' across, (C) is 12' 9", the disfigured cairn (D) 23' 8" north to south but 32' 6" to east to west. The second largest mound (E), the other cairn to have had its centre thrown out, is S17' 6" north to south, while east to west it is 21'. Cairn (F) is 16' in diameter and cairn (G) is 10'.

the dreaded bracken. The width of the cist is seventeen and half inches, although one end stone is leaning inwards, the length can be interpreted as twenty six inches. The cap stone is nowhere to be seen. The whole sits in what remains of its cairn, of which there are a few stones that could be considered as members of the retaining circle. The lie of the cist is 62°NNW.

*　　　*　　　*　　　　　　　　*　　　*　　　*

A little south of the cattle grid at Burcombe Gate the walker will come across a neat little cist. During the warmer months this monument is masked in

To the south, between the rocks of Gutter Tor and the summit of the hill the walker will find the remains of another cist. One can understand why

Gutter Tor cist

Remains of the cist to the south

someone would want to choose this site for their last resting place, for the views are wonderful. However, sadly only one side stone and two different length end stones now survive of the little grave and very little of its cairn. No cap stone is to be seen. Its length is 39" long, each end stone is 20" and 17" respectively. Its lie is 62°NNW.

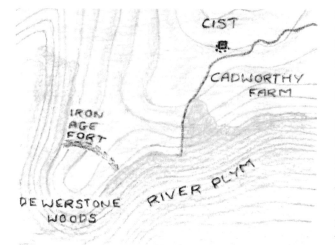

*　　*　　*

Moving now away from the Meavy catchment and into the Plym, I will begin by travelling up the river on its north side, starting high up on Wigford Down. Here a cist sits in the ample remains of its cairn, of which ten stones of its retaining circle still survive more or less in their original positions. Because both side stones are set inside the end stones, both are leaning inwards. Other than that, the cist is in very good condition. Its length is 42", its width is 26" at the bottom, 11" to 12" at the top. Its lie is 52°WWN.

Down a muddy lane at Brisworthy Hamlets can be found a large boulder, now placed into the bottom of a gateway. Shaped into it is a series of cup marks, no one knows for certain what they depict, however, what we do know is that the impressions were the work of Neolithic man. Cups and similar markings can be found on other stones, cists and menhirs around the British Isles. However, to see this boulder's cup marks at their sharpest, it is best

Wigford Down cairn and (inset) the cist

33

The cup stone

buried in the early twentieth century. Although the stones of its make up are not as tall as in other stone circles, the tallest being 57" high, nevertheless it is still quite an impressive spectacle. Very often the Summer Solstice is celebrated here with a fire burning and people singing and dancing.

(2) This cairn circle can be found just out of sight farther up the hill to the north, its present existence is owing, like the stone circle, to another restoration.

(3) This stone row with many stones missing, is related to the cairn circle, which can be seen on the horizon, from which the alignment runs more less to the north, in places it gives away that it was once a double row. Its length is 580 yards

(4) Not so far away to the south-west, the walker will come across this kerb circle. However, not all is what it seems, for a few of the stones have been placed there in recent times to enhance the appearance of the spectacle.

(5) Brisworthy cist. The remains of its cairn is almost unrecognisable as a previous covering mound, yet twelve members of its retaining circle can still be counted, some still in situ, while others have fallen half shrouded in vegetation. Its burial chamber is no doubt one of the best preserved on Dartmoor. Both the side stones and the end stones remain in an upright position with the westernmost made up of two stones. Its huge cap stone was pushed to one side no doubt by those who thought it would be worth the effort, with reward of what might have been buried with the interred. The cist measures 39" one side and 37" on the other, it is 23" wide at one end tapering to 19" at the other. Its lie is 56°NW.

*   *   *

to visit on a clear winter's day when the sun is low in the sky and throwing its rays across the face of the stone.

R. H. Worth not having the advantage of today's knowledge, thought the boulder was a mortar stone from the near by tin workings, describing it as there being nothing else like it anywhere else on Dartmoor.

*   *   *

Above the fields of Brisworthy on Ringmoor Down is a fascinating collection of antiquities for the walker to visit. There is a magnificent stone circle, a cairn circle, a stone row, a kerb circle and a great example of a cist.

(1) Brisworthy stone circle (opposite page top), is seen with Legis Tor in the background. There are stones missing from this monument, no doubt robbed to aid the construction of the near by boundary wall. Like other circles on Dartmoor this one as been restored, most lying prostrate and half

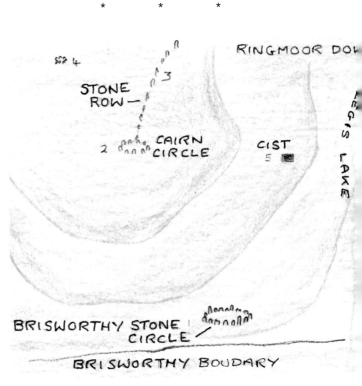

34

BRISWORTHY STONE CIRCLE AND CAIRN CIRCLE

1. Brisworthy stone circle

2. Brisworthy cairn Circle

3. Brisworthy stone row

5. Brisworthy cairn and (below) cist

4. Brisworthy Kerb Circle

LEGIS TOR

Below the salmon-coloured rocks of Legis Tor lie the substantial remains of Prehistoric Enclosures along with their associated hut circles. Ruinus cist and a place the people of their day deposited bones of their dead, those perhaps of less importance to the community. However I must emphasise, the theory of the huge stones being that of an Ossuary is only of my thinking.

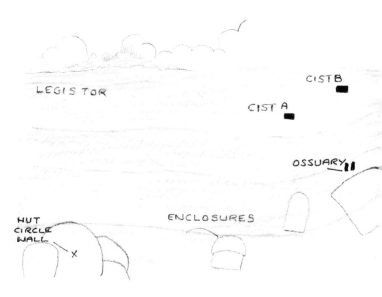

Top: Wall cavity around hut circle, Legis Tor

Above: Entrance door jam to hut circle, Legis Tor

Right: The massive stones of what the author believes might be an ossuary on Legis Tor. This structure is seven feet five inches long on one side and seven feet on the other. It is two feet four inches wide and three feet ten inches deep

Below: The capstone of cist A

Only two side stones remain of cist A and even those have been badly disturbed while it was robbed of its end stones. For at one end it measures 23" while at the other, it is 28". The length of the side stones are 27" and 35" respectively. The presence of the cap stone can be found resting on the mound of the much dilapidated cairn. There are many stones that could well pass as members of a retaining circle. The cist's lie, taken from the longest side stone, is 51°WNW.

*Legis Tor ruined cairn B
and (inset) cist*

Legis Tor B is again a much ruined cairn and cist with only one side stone measuring 30″ and one end stone measuring 19″. Its lie is 61°NNW. The cap stone can be seen half buried in the side of what remains of the cairn.

*   *   *

The Drizzlecombe complex, like that of the Merrivale site, is much visited by those that are interested in prehistory and also those that choose to peruse the unusual. Here there are stone rows and their menhirs, cists, a kerb circle, and cairns.

This menhir stands at the outset of stone row (B) and it, like the other two menhirs, was once pros-

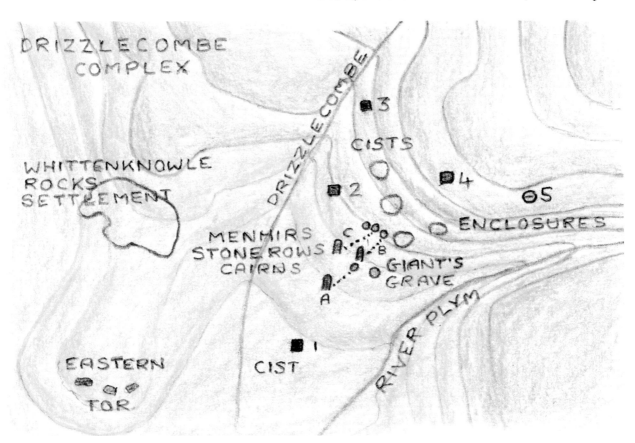

Enclosures and hut circles on the hill above the stone rows and kistvaens

trate lying among the moorland vegetation until , in 1893, R. H. Worth and his team of enthusiasts had it secured in concrete so it could stand regally in its vertical position once more. In 1889, whilst the stone lay on the ground, Mr Worth measured it at 17' 10". It now stands at 14', the tallest menhir on Dartmoor. The nodule at top of the stone is purely the natural seam split of the granite.

Drizzlecombe Menhir row B

Left: The fallen menhir

Below: With Menhirs at the heads of their stone rows (A) farthest away, and (B)

Above left: Drizzlecombe Menhir of Row A is 10ft 6in

Above right: The smallest Menhir C, 7ft 9in

Below left: Row B is quite unlike the other two in that it runs double for a few yards

Below: Row C has some of the smallest stones

The Giant's Basin.

Cist A

Cist C

Each stone row has a cairn at its north-east end; another cairn sits in line those of (B) and (C). There are other cairns within the Drizzlecombe complex the largest being that of the huge so called 'Giant's Basin'. This great stone mound, now shrouded in vegetation and surrounded by reeds, has been dug into to a fair depth by those hoping to find their efforts rewarded. The monument according to R.H. Worth is 71' across, 10' high and it had been delved into to a depth of 6' 6".

There are three cists to be perused while strolling in the valley. Cist (A) can be found as one enters the complex from the track that passes the dwelling of Ditsworthy Warren house. After fording the Drizzlecombe Brook it can be found by walking to the north-east. Only two side stones standing well above the ground and a slab lying close by that could have been an end stone, is all that remains of this cist. The much smaller stones to be found in the floor at each end of the cist, I think are trig stones that once held the end stones in place. The absence of a cairn could be down to the tin work-

ings close by, convenient material to be ground down for their mineral content. To give some idea of the size of the cist, the stone measure 58" and 61". Its width is 23" tapering to 19" its lie is 52°WNW.

Cist (B) is the complete burial chamber, the two huge side stones and end stones stand upright with its cap stone leaning over all. The interior of the cist measures are 42" long 29" wide. Its lie is 56°NW, all set in the large area of its cairn.

Cist (C) is devoid of its cairn no doubt the result of the tinners having worked close by in the Drizzlecombe Brook. Here, like Cist B, all four stones protrude above the ground. It's a shame that the cap stone is not there to complete the little monument. Its dimensions are 36" long by 26" wide. Its lie is 56°NW.

Cist B

Cist D

Cist E

There are question marks against two other that are thought to be possible cists.

The first (D) sits above the enclosures, at approximately SX 595 687. The feature sits in a depression surrounded by raised ground, with one seemingly set stone lined precisely north-west. At one time the stone lying beside it was earth-fast.

(E) this stone is set in the hollow of a substantial cairn. Its lie is 46°WSW 14°ENE. This could make it an end stone, giving licence to imagine a side stone to lie 1°NNE 33°SSE, in true cist fashion.

*   *   *

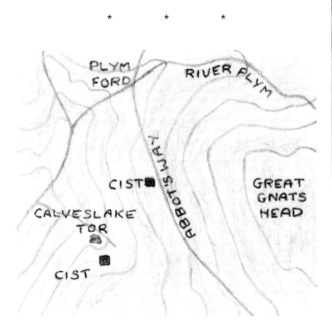

On the opposite side of the River Plym lies the peak of Great Gnats Head. Below it lying to the west of the Abbot's Way can be found the three stones of a cist. The side stones stand upright, while the one end stone lies prostrate on the ground between them. All lie in the hollow of what remains of their covering cairn. The side stones measure in length 44" and 38" respectively, the width between them is 29" at their bottoms. The lie of the cist is more less east-west.

Centre: The Abbot's Way cist

Above: The three stones of the Abbot's Way cist

Calves Lake cist

Inset: The capstone

Calves Lake cist lies well down in its cairn, all five stones still exist. The cap stone leans on one corner. The internal measurements of the cist are 42″ long by 24″ wide. Its lie is 56°NW.

*   *   *

The Langcombe Brook is the most cist-populated tributary stream on the moor, eleven altogether, including cist (G) which I think in the most spectacular grave on Dartmoor. Cist (A) is almost completely covered by its cap stone; there are a couple of places where one can feel the stones of the cist, it seem that two side stones and one end stone are in place, but true measurements are not possible to ascertain. Its lie is 58°NW.

Upper Deadman's Bottom cist

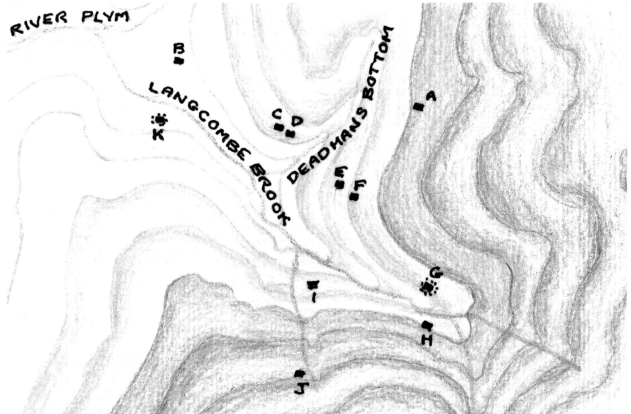

Lancombe Cist B and (inset) a close-up view

Cist (B) of salmon-pink coloured granite, is in very good condition. Both side and end stones are in situ with the cap stone leaning against one of the sides. The internal measurements of the cist are 33" at one side and 31" at the other. Its width is 21" tapering to 14". The remains of the cairn which is not substantial, shows only three members of the retaining circle. The lie of the cist is 57°NW.

Cist (C) is in a mess; the years have not treated it kindly, or should we assume it's man who is the culprit of its sad decline. One side stone is the only section of the cist that is upright, the other leans owing to the weight of the heavy cap stone bearing on it. Only one end stone exist and that lies at an angle from its true position. To get some idea of the size of the cist one side stone is 46" in length while its opposite number is 42". The lie of the sad little monument is 53°WNW.

Only a few yards away from (C) can be seen cist (D) sitting in the remains of its cairn which still has half a dozen retaining stones protecting its northeastern extremity. The cist has only three stones in place, one side stone and two end stones. If the missing side stone was in place and spanned across the extremities like that of the one in situ, the width of the cist would be 28". Its length is 38". Its related cap stone lies within the confines of the cairn. The lie of the cist is 58°NNW.

Lancombe Cist C and (inset) a close-up view

Above: Langcombe Cist D and (inset) Cist D in the landscape. Below: Cist E and (below right) Cist E in the landscape

Cist (E), on the other side of the Deadmans Bottom stream, will in a few years time be hidden from view encompassed within mass of tussocky ground. When I first located this grave in the early 1970s, its stones were proud of the turf. Now just portions of their tops faintly appear through the moorland moss and grass that manages to grow in and around the stones.

Measurements that can be ascertained, reveal there is 50" of one side stone, and 25" across the cist. The whole sits on very little of a cairn. However the cist lie can be recorded at, 54°NNW.

Cist (F) sits in an insignificant little mound of a cairn about fifty walking paces uphill to the southeast from the sad remains of the previous specimen. This little feature can be spotted in an oases of sheep-nibbled grass that is surrounded by many square acres of tussocky ground. Far more of this grave can be seen but how long for is down to the elements. Both side stones protrude above the ground. However, although one end stone can be seen leaning inwards, its opposite number being covered in a thick layer of moss can only be felt. 27" by 18" is the size of the cist. Its lie is 55°NW.

Below: Cist F and (below right) Cist F in the landscape

Above: Langcombe Cist G, Grim's Grave and (right) the cist close up

Cist (G), Grim's Grave, is the only specimen on the moor that is given a name, but where it stems from, now no one is sure. For me it is without doubt the most impressive cist on the moor. The grave is surrounded by a circle comprising nine large boulders; no other grave on the moor can boast of such protection. The only disadvantage it has as a spectacle is that its cap stone is missing, however in saying that, there is a slab of granite in the bottom of the cist that could well have been one of perhaps two that formed the cover. The cist itself measures 41" one side, 37" on the other, its width is 31" tapering to 29". Its lie is 1°N.

Cist (H) can be seen across the Langcombe Brook with its cap stone sitting askew on top of it. With one end stone missing its length cannot be measured exactly, but the width can and is 23" at one end tapering to 20" at the other. All sit in the centre of the substantial remains of its cairn. I do think that a re-excavation of this monument might discover the stones of an inner and outer circle. Its lie is 50°WNW.

Cist (I) is another that could well disappear from our view within a few years if care is not afforded to it, it is sometimes difficult to locate where it is situated among a large acreage of tussocky ground. When I first photographed it, three of its stones could be seen showing well above ground level, now only one end stone is clear of the turf. However it measurements can be ascertained; they are 29" along one side and 28" on the other, while its width is 26" tapering to 23". There is no sign of its cap stone and its cairn is almost non-existent. Its lie is 50°WNW.

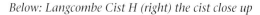

Below: Langcombe Cist H (right) the cist close up

Below: Langcombe Cist I (right) the cist close up

Above: Langcombe Cist J close up and (above right) the cist in the landscape

Above: Langcombe Cist K close up and (above right) the cist in the landscape

Cist (J) is the highest grave sited on the Langcombe Brook watershed, With views over the Walkham Tors, it can be found on the left bank of a tributary of the Langcombe. It sits in the remains of a substantial cairn with a few stones of its retaining circle to be identified. With one end stone missing the length of the cist cannot be ascertained exactly. The width however measures 21" tapering to 19", with the cap stone resting on one of the side stones. Its lie is 54°WNW.

When first looking at Cist K one could be excused if one's thoughts took it to be a double cist, and even a close inspection doesn't satisfy the mind completely for there is a third elongated stone running parallel to the cist. Maybe it was designed to be a future double which never came to fruition. The cap stone sits on what is left of its cairn.

All four stones of the cist are still in place, its measurements are 49" on one side and 42" on the other, while its width is 20" tapering to 14". Its lie is 61°NNW.

*　　　*　　　*

On Giant's Hill a little south of the smallest enclosure, and just below the old Phillips' china clay leat will be found the next prehistoric features.

47

Possible cist on Giant's Hill

Underneath the slab

This feature needs to be excavated before it can be scheduled as a cist. However, what I think is a cap stone lies on top of a slight mound. Pushing a tape to measure beneath the slab touched a stone at the far end of the cavity. The distance when I pulled the tape out again was 22", not knowing what exactly I was measuring I am afraid the lie of the feature could not be ascertained.

The photograph above right shows the underneath side of the slab and either one end stone and a side stone (and a nest, perhaps of a mouse!).

This scheduled cist was unknown to me until I actually walked into it one morning when thick cloud suddenly came down on to the surface of the moor. The cist sits in an oasis of sheep-nibbled grass, exposed to the elements with both side

stones and two end stones showing just above the turf. The other end stone is leaning inward, almost prostrate. However, the length of the cist 25" could be measured by mentally placing the leaning end stone in its original vertical position. The width is 18" tapering to 14". Its lie is 3°NNE. There is very little evidence of a cairn.

* * *

*Site of the scheduled cist on Giant's Hill with
(inset) the cist stones*

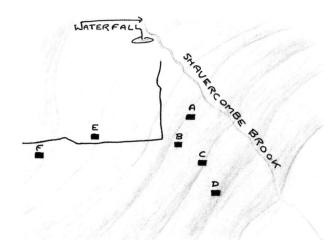

Cist B

Above the small but beautiful waterfall on the Shavercombe Brook, can be found a cemetery of Bronze Age cists. It lies between the brook and the ruins of Hen Tor Farm.

Cist A

Cist (A) sadly lies hidden among a dense area of tussocky moorland. One side stone, being a great deal longer, is placed outside the end stones while its smaller opposite number is placed between. It has an internal length of 30" on one side and 27" on the other. Its width is 16" tapering to 14". Its lie is 57°NW.

Cist (B) lies a few yards above the corner of the Hen Tor Warren Farm boundary hedge in the remains of its small cairn. Most of the cist can be seen showing just above the turf; all of it is there including its cap stone that could well be the half buried slab near the lower fringes of the cairn. The cist measures 30" on one side and 27" on the other. Its width 16" tapering to 14". The lie is 57°NW.

Cist (C) can be found uphill to the south-east among the tussocks. The cist, in ruins, sits in the quite impressive remains of its cairn that still has a great deal of its retaining circle in place. However the state of the cist rather lets the whole thing down. Both side stones that were set inside the end stones lean inward. One end stone can be clearly seen, but its opposite number cannot. However there is a stone that can be felt, but it is hidden behind thick vegetation. To give some idea of its size the one end stone is 21" long and one side stone measures 40". Its lie is again 57°NW.

Below: The view over Cist B

The view across Cist C with (inset) the cist stones

Cist (D) is another wreck of a cist. It is situated again up hill in a mire of bracken, stone and soggy ground. This cist is a complete ruin, sitting in the centre of its moss-shrouded cairn. One end stone is missing and the one that is there is hidden in vegetation and both side stones are quite out of place. Sadly owing to the state of the cist no measurements can be taken. However to give some idea of its size one side stone measures 58″ in length. Adding to the whole sorry state the cap stone has forlornly slipped into the cavity's centre. The lie of the cist is 57°NW.

Cist (E) lies a couple of hundred yards to the west of Cist (B,) just inside the field boundary hedge of Hen Tor Farm. This odd little feature is set in the remains of a small cairn, only one side stone and two end stones of different lengths have stood the test of time. I am sure that one side was once made up of two stones seeing one end stone measures 15″ and the other only 7″. One can assume that if the missing side stone held a position like that of the existing one, and the small end stone had a companion, the width of the cist would have been 15″. Its length is 26″. It has a lie of 53°WNW.

Cist (F) again is ruinous, consisting of only one end stone and two side stones, all three barely showing above the turf. The width can be determined at 28″ tapering to 26″. With the one end stone missing the length can not be measured. Its lie is 5°NNE.

The much ruined Cist D and (inset) the cap stone of Cist D showing it lying in the cavity

Above: The view across Cist E with (below left) the cist stones

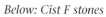

Below: Cist F stones

Willingswalls Reave.

51

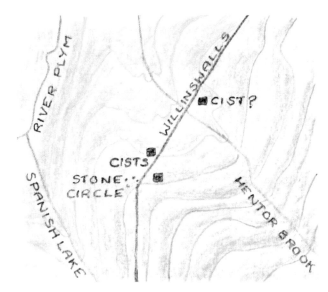

A possible cist site can be found a few yards from the prehistoric reave of Willingswalls, sixty paces north-east of the Hen Tor Brook. What may be one end stone and one side stone which is 30" long. Its lie is 50°WNW.

The first of the Willingswalls cists that have been scheduled. All four stones of the cist can be seen within the confines of its ragged cairn, but one side stone lies almost on its side, resting at an angle a foot away on the floor. The whole is situated on the west side of the reave. If the dislodged side stone was back in its original place, positioned like its partner (for it is long enough), the width of the cist would be 21" tapering to 18"; its length is 30". Its lie is 56°NW. The cap stone lies half buried to the west on the side of the cairn.

Although a little untidy, the monument in the photo (top of the page following) is most stunning, although spoiling the cist are the two end stones that are leaning inward, otherwise it's perfect. To give some idea of its size one side stone that the huge cap stone leans on, measures 5' 7", while the width of its chamber is 3' 1". Its lie is 51°WNW. There are eight large stones of its cairns retaining circle remaining.

This circle comprising five groups of stones, is situated on the brow of the hill to the west of Willingswalls Reave, in fact one is incorporated in the reave itself. R.H. Worth first brought this feature to our attention in 1942, saying he thought it was an unusual circle. It has a diameter of about 140 feet. If it is a true circle, the reave runs through its eastern side. Here speculation enters one's thoughts, for was the reave built at a later age than the circle, or did the circle builders, for some strategically advantageous positioning, need to place their creation right here? We can only ponder on such questions.

Possible cist above Hentor Brook

The first of the Willingswalls cists (inset)
lies within its ragged cairn

Above: The massive cap stone leans on the side stone of the second Willingwalls cist

Left: The remains of the second cist

Below: The circle comprising five groups of stones

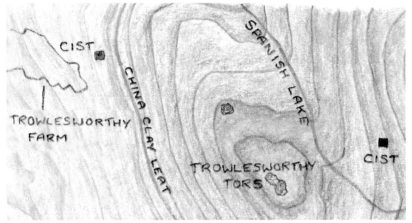

have fallen; the tallest of those that may be standing is 14" high. There are stones on the higher elevation of the circumference that confuse the picture as to the layout of a true circle. Whether the slight depression in the centre of the ring is man made or natural is also very much open to question.

Up on the hill above the fields of Trowlesworthy Farm, just below the China Clay Leat, situated among a conglomeration of large stones and boulders, is the sad remains of a cist. Although the hillside is littered with prehistoric remains, including two stone rows, this is the only grave to be found on the hill. One side was originally made up

Above: View over Spanish Lake cist. Below: The cist stones

The stone enclosure near the Warren bound

The Spanish Lake cist is a neat Burial Chamber and can be found 140 walking paces up the gently sloping hillside to the east of the huge No.1 Hentor Warren huge bound stone. Its four stones sit near the edge of the cairn rather than in its centre. Both side and end stones are in their original positions, much as they were when first put in place. The cist is 26" long and 25" wide tapering to 24". No cap stone can be seen. Its lie is 50°WNW.

This intriguing stone circle lies more or less north-west of the warren bound stone, below an enclosure that appears to be divided in two. Its diameter measures 29' 8" and 24 stones can be counted in its circumference. Most look as if they

of two stones the longest, as the photograph (inset on following page) shows, is now missing, the empty space measures 32". The remaining small piece is 6" long making the length if the side was complete 37", the side still in situ, is 33" long. The width of the cist is 19". The large hump-shaped cap stone has been manoeuvered to the edge of the ruined cairn, of which eleven stones of its retaining circle remain. The lie of the cist is 63°NNW.

Shaugh Moor stone row stretches out to the north-east from a retaining circle. It lies to the west of Beatland Corner to Cadover Bridge road about 200 or so yards from the ancient Shaden Cross. All the stones are small and short in height with several missing or buried over the centuries by the moorland turf. The single stone row, according to Worth, stretches for approximately 190 yards to the last surviving stone, one of rather insignificant size compared to other terminators, unless a larger stone has been removed from its position before Mr Worth's time. I would say he was right in concluding that this stone is the termination of the row, for since his day the china clay industry has spread a great acreage of waste over the site.

On the south-western slopes of Shaugh Moor is the rock pile of Hawks Tor; the rocks are undoubtedly those of a tor. However, I don't think it can be dismissed lightly to suggest the tor was utilised

*The cap stone and (inset) the
cist in the fields above Trowlesworthy Farm*

Shaugh Moor stone row

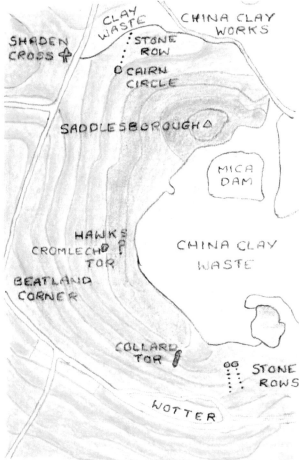

as a dolmen, a cromlech, for this is what it was once thought to be, proof of which can be seen on the old map below. While modern thought may contradict this theory there is little evidence to disprove the earlier interpretation.

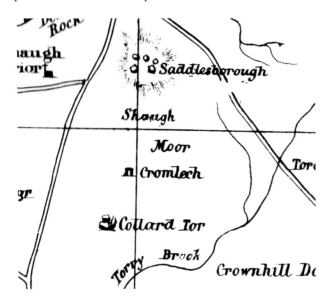

When one takes a look at the Kilclooney dolmen in Count Donegal in Ireland, one can see a distinct resemblance. For it, like the feature on Hawks Tor, has employed a smaller boulder to give the cap stone a more level and higher elevation.

The other noticeable feature of Hawks Tor cover stone is that this huge stone of many tons, has been turned. It was once no doubt part of the main section of the tor. For if one notices the grain of the granite it has been clearly manoeuvered around and away from its original position and allowed to come to rest on the introduction of a small boulder that sits on the smaller rock pile. If one looks at the grain in the great slab it is evident that it runs at

Top: Hawks Tor 'dolmen'

Above: The Kilclooney dolmen in Ireland

right angles to the grain on the tor itself. The Roof Slab is 18' 2" long by 10' 2" wide. The internal dimensions of the cavity is 10' 4" deep by 6' 2" wide and the height to the roof is 6' 10".

One of the stone rows above Wotter

The second stone row above Wotter.

On the southern edge of Shaugh Moor, overlooking the houses of Wotter, are two stone rows running alongside each other. They are unusual in that their alignment runs through a boulder-strewn terrain. Excuses could be made if the unknowing eye was to pass by without noticing them; both are quite ruinous with some of their members missing. The cairn at the head of the row nearest to Collard Tor is not so distinctive as its neighbour that displays a circle of stones.

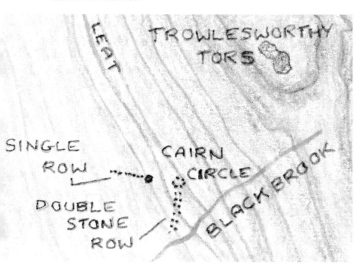

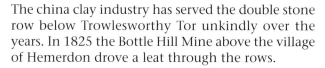

The china clay industry has served the double stone row below Trowlesworthy Tor unkindly over the years. In 1825 the Bottle Hill Mine above the village of Hemerdon drove a leat through the rows.

Above right: Looking down the double row from the bank of the china clay leat

Right: Looking up the double row towards the Pulpit Circle from the bank of the leat

TROWLESWORTHY STONE ROWS

The Pulpit: the double row's stone circle

The tallest member of the double row has at sometime in the distant past fallen; it measures from end to end, lying on the ground, 84". The double row did not only suffer loss from the leat, but at the bottom end of the alignments one can surmise that some of its members are missing, for there doesn't appear to be a true termination, the likes of a blocking stone, that are found on most other stone rows.

Its cairn, like that of the double row, lies up the slope at its eastern end. There are in this row, like the double row, stones missing. The situation with these two alignments is unusual in that they run at different angles, with the single row running east to west, while the double runs north to south.

Above: The Single stone row below the Leat with its blocking stone

Below: The Pulpit at sunset

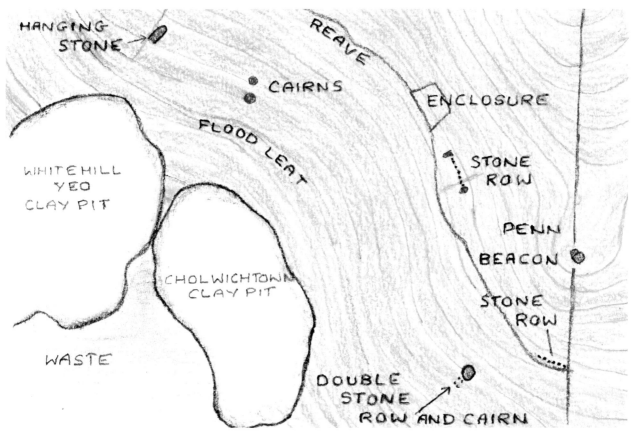

Hanging Stone bound stone

The tumbled stones of the chambered cairn

The first artefact of prehistory we see while trekking across the escarpment below the heights of Shell Top and Penn Beacon is the Hanging Stone. It can be found beside a dyke, a couple of hundred yards uphill from the flood trench that takes water away from the china clay pits of Whitehill Yeo and Cholwichtown. Etched on its eastern side, are the initials CB in capital letters telling the curious that it was once utilised as a bound stone by the owners of the ancient Cholwichtown estate. The whole leans at a peculiar angle, that is to say it not only leans a little to the north-west but also a little to the north-east.

A little further on towards the south-east can be seen a huge pile of stones. This was once a quite large chambered cairn that over the years has been robbed of many of its stones, distorting it grossly out of shape. It appears that in the recent past some one, or perhaps a group, has reshaped the north-east section of the structure as it can clearly be seen that the area has been worked over. The original stones have been deliberately placed rather than thrown, with the work covering a small chamber that aims towards the centre of the cairn, its di-

A view over the Chamered cairn

The passage into the cairn at Shell Top

The possible cist stone in the cairn

mensions are 8″ high by 8″ wide. The length, so far as I have been able to measure it, is difficult to obtain as my measure kept snagging on something about three feet into this intriguing feature.

On the western side of the cairn just over 20′ from the edge of the 83′ wide structure, is a set stone 37″ long that I think could well be the side stone of a cist. Its lie is 7°NE 39°SW. On the other hand the stone could well be the remains of the chamber that Worth discovered and describes in his book.

*   *   *

Further along the escarpment uphill to the east, can be found a stone row discovered by the author in October 1992. Difficult to locate now the moorland vegetation has been allowed to shroud it again, it lies to the south-east of the settlement that sits above the line of Lee Moor–Penn Moor boundary stones. The three photographs on the following page correspond with the drawing I made not many days after I went back to measure and photographed sections of the row. The cairn which lies at the eastern end of the row is almost oval in shape and the stones in the row leading away from it seems to have been thrown out with only half a

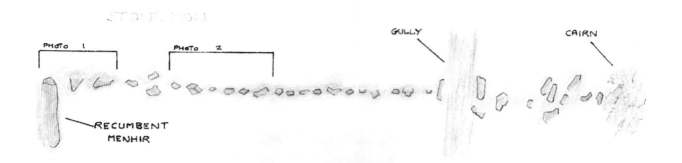

The next feature we examine, while trying to avoid the wet ground created by spring water, lies to the south of this alignment. In summer during a spell of dry weather this obstacle can be negotiated without to much bother, but generally it is best to skirt around the higher ground above it then drop downhill (over the reave) for a few contours until reaching a cairn comprising a huge mass of grey granite stones. Here again the contents have been badly disturbed, and stones thrown anywhere to satisfy the mind of those that needlessly and ignorantly want to ruin. Many of the stones have been robbed from the pile (no doubt employed for the stone walling of the fields below), like those of the double stone row that is much dilapidated, with only four stones remaining of its run down the hill, How long ago the stones of the row were taken, history doesn't record. Any impression they may have left in the moorland surface is impossible to trace without the aid of excavation, perhaps to reveal trig stones and other evidence of their existence.

dozen still in their original place. Spoiling the alignment still further is a gully running through it, from which most the stones are more or less in place with the majority still standing, with a good few coated in vegetation. The monument's terminating stone (top photo) lies at right angles to the row, lying at an angle suggesting that its thin edge once looked along the stones. The length of the row is two hundred and thirty four feet. It lies, give or take a few feet, is twenty seven yards uphill from the reave that runs along the escarpment below.

Penn Moor south double stone row and cairn

61

Top: Penn stone row looking east

Above: Penn stone row looking west

Not far to the north of east from the large cairn and the remains of the double row, just above the reave that runs along the escarpment, can be found yet another much dilapidated monument, a stone row. It runs to the reave that climbs steeply up to Penn Beacon before travelling on up to Shell Top. There may be other stones in the alignment that lie beneath the turf but only ten stones of varying heights have survived to show themselves above it, with members running in a haphazard fashion along from east to west on level ground. No evidence can be seen that the row runs beyond the reave. Also nothing remains of what may have been an associated cairn or a terminal blocking stone at the end of the sixty-six foot long monument.

Following the reave up the steep incline will bring the interested walker to Penn Beacon where two cairns can be surveyed. The lower of the two displays what could be the ruins of a chambered cairn; there are two seemingly set stones on the higher side of the ruin, one at each end, and both facing 5°NNE. There is another prominent seemingly set stone, towards the north end of the ruin as if running to its centre, facing in the same direction as the two previously mentioned stones, again providing some evidence that we might be looking at the ruins of a chambered cairn.

The stones of the more prominent and far larger structure, that sits on the very peak of the hill, has over the years been transformed into a shelter from the elements (now roofless).

Not a lot can be seen of the cairn's original retaining circle, except the two set stones on its northern edge and the two huge stones of boulder proportions, one leaning against the other on the structure's south-eastern edge, with the upright stone standing three feet in height, from where there appears to be two lines of stones running in towards the bowels of the great mound.

*   *   *

Penn Beacon cairn looking south

Penn Beacon ruinous cairn and (inset) the two set stones

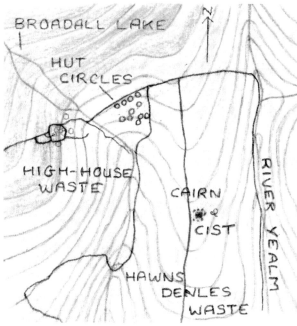

Hut circle door jambs

Now we move into the valley of the Yealm. Here can be viewed the largest and most magnificent pair of prehistoric door jambs to be seen on Dartmoor. They can be found within the confines of High-House Waste, which can be found to the ENE of Penn Beacon. The ground is now in the ownership of the Dartmoor Preservation Association.

The stone pillar on the left of the picture above stands at a height of 4' 8", its width is 1' 11" inches and it is 1' 3" thick. The giant, its partner stands at 4' 9" while its width is 2'9" and its thickness is 11". These door jambs fronted a hut circle that whose floor was raised on the downhill side to make it level. Very little stonework remains of the dwelling, most of it no doubt robbed for the field wall that can be seen near the top of the photograph. The hut ruin sits in the midst of others all free-standing, and not surrounded by the usual enclosure.

Hut circle below High-House Waste

Almost in view of the door jambs, is the cairn circle and cist that sits in the ground of Hawns and Dendles Waste. Only the two side stones remain to be seen today, the end stones are nowhere to be found. The length of the largest side stone is 56" while that of its opposite number cannot be ascertained owing to it being partly buried in vegetation. However the width between the two stones is 27". Nine good size stones make up the cairn circle. The whole not so very long ago sat under the shade of a forest of conifers. The lie of the cist is 50°WNW. No cap stone can be found.

Cairn circle in Hawns and Dendles Waste.

Cist No.2 above Ranny Brook

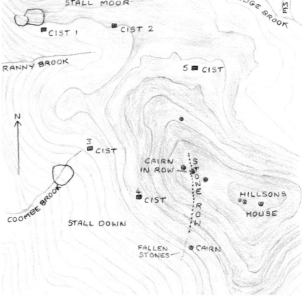

The stones of the Ranny Brook Cist No.1

Close to the twin enclosures on the edge of Stall Moor, just a couple of hundred yards above the Ranny Brook, near the right hand bottom corner of the largest enclosure, can be found the ruins of a cist. Only two stones remain today, along with what could be a couple of trig stones (small stones used to hold the cist's sides in place). Where the missing stones went we can only speculate, but they could well have been taken by the tin miners who in past centuries excavated the gullys nearby.

Nothing remains of the cist's burial mound and there is no sign of its cap stone. The inner measurement of the longer side stone is 29" while the end stone measures 19". The lie of the grave is 61°NNW.

A couple of hundred yards to the east of No.1 cist can be found the remains of No.2 cist, no doubt contorted into the shape it is today through the passage of three thousand and more years. One side

stone looks to be sitting in its original position, while its opposite number and the one end stone stand askew. At the other end of the grave are two small stones wedged into the ground. These I think are trig stones, placed there to help prop up the original end stone, holding it in place (if indeed there was ever one there at all). One side measures 31" while the other measures 27". It is 16" wide at one end tapering to 14" at the other. Its lie is 51°WNW. No mound of a cairn nor its cap stone can be found.

Ranny Brook east cist No.2 and (inset) the stones of the cist.

Cist No.3 can be found still buried in its cairn above the head mire of the Coomb Brook. Like No.2 one end stone is missing. An earth-fast boulder is utilised for one side. The other side stone leans inward, and one end stone that also slants, stops it collapsing. Owing to its state, the true dimensions of the grave can not be ascertained. Its lie is 55°NW. no cap stone is to be found.

It is a walk of about a third of a mile uphill to the SSE to the ruins of cist No.4. It lies on the side of the Down with fabulous views out over the in-country. The grid reference of its location is SX628623. Only one side stone and one end stone can now be seen, and even these are mostly layered in moss. To give some idea of its size, the side stone measures 51″ and the end stone is 20″ in length. Both lie in the confines of their ruined cairn of which three stones are visible of its circle. No cap stone is to be found.

The grave's lie is 50°WNW.

Ranny Brook cist 3 and (inset) the stones of the cist.

STALL DOWN

The view across No.4 cist and (inset) the stones of cist 4

The next point of interest spreads itself across the top of the Down from the valley of the Yealm to the valley of the Erme. It is one of the most majestic alignments the walker will come across on Dartmoor, yet it is also the cause of great intrigue and confusion. A cairn that lies about two hundred yards to the south of it, is one of the features that has in the past led people the reach a conclusion that the alignment should have pointed in that direction and not the way in which the antiquarian the Rev. Sabine Baring-Gould and his team directed during restoration in the last decade of the nineteenth century, despite the contention that they placed the stones back in the holes they had fallen out of. The photo below shows the stone row running up hill from its bottom end, that is to say in

Stall Down stone row

The four fallen stones on Stall Down

The ruined cairn

the valley of the Yealm. The photo above, shows four of the twenty-three stones that have fallen to the south of the stone row. The end stone or blocking stone of this sad row also lies prostrate and is six foot in length. Sixty-three stones still stand resultant from the work that Baring-Gould carried out while twenty five-have again fallen.

Near the top of the alignment is a feature that has caused a difference of opinion. Like the north row at Merrivale it has a cairn interrupting the line of the row. The photo above right shows the dilapidated cairn with the stone row that has climbed the hill, finishing on the left, then carrying on over into Erme country on its right. The giants of the row are found on this side of the hill, the tallest being 7' 6" high. The last two are found beyond the giants overlooking the valley of the Erme

West of the tallest standing stone in the row can be found a cairn with four stones still standing of its inner retaining circle and ten stones of its outer circle of which six are still standing.

A glance to the south-east, sitting on the crown of the Down, the walker will see another cairn. Erected with some of the stones of the huge monument are the three surviving walls of a building. Here so the story tells us, lived a fellow by the name of Hillson who apparently made eight-day clocks.

Directly to the North lying among acres of heather and tussocky ground can be found an oasis of sheep-nibbled grass. Situated within this oasis is a cairn with a neat little cist set more or less in its centre. Only two side stones and one end stone remain; the width of the cist tapers from 27" to 21". Without the end stone its length can not be determined. Its lie is 59°NNW.

No cap stone can be found but five stones of the cairn circle are still to be seen; others could well be buried.

The tallest stones on Stall Down

The photos above shows the longest of the two fallen stones which measures nine feet four inches, the stone on the right is seven feet long by three feet wide.

The cairn on the crown of Stall Down and (inset below left) a closer view of Hillson's building

The cairn lying to the north and (inset above) the stones of the cist

69

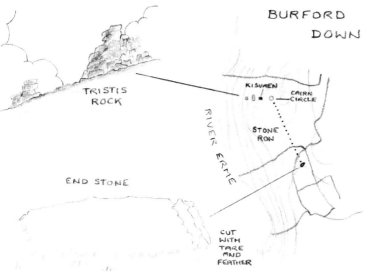

The Burford Down cairn and (inset below) the side stone of the cist

We are now in the valley of the Erme. Just over a mile, from the Yealm-end of the recognised stone row, at a little to the east of west, can be located another alignment. It runs down the northern slope of Burford Down. Its outset begins with a ruined cairn that still displays seven members of its retaining circle and ends (after being sliced in two by a stone wall) with a large stone which lies prostrate on the ground with a section cut out of it by the old method of stonecutting, feather and tare.

A stroll of a few yards to the east, towards Tristis Rock, can be found another cairn with ten stones of its retaining circle still in place. The rest of the make up of the monument has been robbed of its stones, no doubt like its neighbour, to be used elsewhere In the centre of the cairn can be seen one side stone of a cist. To give some idea of its size. the length of the stone is 4' 7", standing 12" proud of the ground. Its lie is 51°WNW.

It's a long walk beside the River Erme before fording of the Blatchford Brook and a steady climb up the south-east slope of Stall Moor to reach the next item of interest. It is a stone circle with the name of The Dancers attached to it. The quite impressive circle fronts a stone row two miles long, supposedly the longest in the world.

Like a lot of stone circles, There is a story to be told about it. The tale tells the yarn of a young boy and several young maidens gleefully strolling, occasionally skipping merrily, prancing over the moor. The sun was high, warming a clear summer day and a gentle cool breeze blew quivering the new tender green growth of the heather. They stopped a little above the river where the cattle graze, and lay in the grass for a while, the girls giggled and whispered and started to sing, then up on their feet and danced in a ring. Suddenly, the sun went from the sky, encouraging the boys to tease, then silence fell upon the moor and the cool breeze lost its tone. Then a vast flash of light lit all around, turning the girls into stone. Apparently for dancing on a Sunday!

The Burford Down stone row

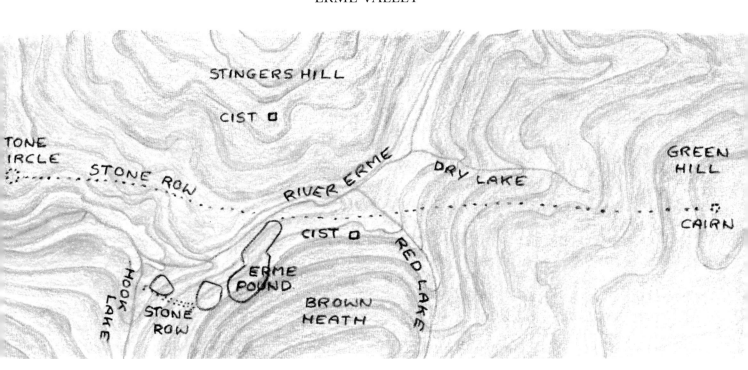

The outset of the stone row above the Erme

The row running down to Green Lake

The Dancers stone circle

The row looking out from Green Lake

Material other than granite was used

Stone exposed by peat cutting

The row on the way down to the Erme

The row as it crosses Brown Heath

The ruined cairn on Green Hill

The cairn on Stingers Hill and (inset) the cist

Some yards west of the stone row on Stingers Hill a cairn looks down on Erme Pound. The cairn has within its midst a ruined cist; its true dimensions are impossible to ascertain as only one side stone remains which is 60" long. One end appears to be made up of two stones, the other end stone is missing; perhaps it is the one standing on its edge in the middle of the chamber. The cist's lie is 50°WNW.

Seven stones of the cairn's retaining circle still stand in position albeit leaning this way or that. The photograph above was taken in the summer of 1989; on seeing the amount of erosion one feared for its wellbeing. However, a visit after the foot and mouth outbreak when fewer livestock were allowed on the moor, it seems to have recovered from its sad condition.

Just a few yards uphill to the east of the stone row as it progresses across Brown Heath can be found one of the most complete cists on the moor. It sits in the tussock-covered mound of its cairn looking down on the Erme and its confluence with the Red Lake. Its dimensions are 43" long and 26" wide. At the time of measuring there was a layer of silt over its base with a good few inches of water covering it, the depth of the cist from the top of the side walls is 2' 6". Its lie is 54°WNW. As the photograph shows the cap stone has survived and has been dragged to one side for the purpose of excavation in times gone by.

The cist on Brown Heath and (below) its interior

73

Also on Brown Heath there is a double stone row. It lies on the far side of Erme Pound, a large prehistoric enclosure that has, in more modern times, been employed as a livestock drifting pound. The double row can be found running away from a dilapidated cairn (top picture) which lies on the south-east edge of the enclosure situated to the south of the large pound.

In William Crossing's day a ruined cist could be found amidst the stones of the cairn. There are a dozen stones of its circle to be counted, with ten still standing, one being 4' 10" high, one fallen and sadly others missing or buried.

Crossing made the length of the row 170 yards. However, it seems as if this gentleman took his measurement up to a small extension of a smaller enclosure that lies to the north of Hook Lake, and wasn't aware of a couple of stones that I am sure were originally members of the row and, judging by their shape, may have actually been the row's blocking stones. They can be located just a couple of yards from the very edge of the deep tinners' workings that the waters of Hook Lake help to create. A fascinating thing about this double alignment is that on its way down the hill, just a few yards from the cairn, it scrapes the edge of a hut circle before running on for several yards more and interfering with the side of the enclosure. The stones in the row vary considerably in size from merely displaying their heads above the turf to being over three feet in height.

Another double stone row can be found almost two miles away on Piles Hill. However, all but three of its members lie prostrate on the ground, some cut revealing the scars of the feather and tare cutting process. Many have fallen and are half hidden by a covering of moorland vegetation while others are completely shrouded with the same, and many are missing altogether.

The Brown Heath enclosure

The double stone row

The double stone row as it ascends the hill

The standing blocking stone and its fallen partner

If the remains of this row and those stones that have been mutilated or have been taken away were standing in place it would be a monument to compare with any other in Britain. It stretches for over half a mile across the saddle of Piles Hill with one end looking down into the Erme and the other end overlooking the Glaze Brook. 64' 4" separates the two rows at the Erme end, while 62' 3" separate them at the Glaze Brook.

The Erme end of the northern row finishes with two blocking stones, in similar fashion to those in the north row at Merrivale. One of these stones lies almost prostrate while its partner at 6' 2" leans uphill towards the stones of the row. However, those who might be tempted to compare these stones to those of the Carnac alignments in Brittany can never have been anywhere near those ancient Breton monuments.

Recumbent member of the southern row split by stone cutters

Ten foot stone beside the old Red Lake rail bed

Partly shrouded, split and eroded stone in the southern row

Two partly buried stones in the southern row

PILES HILL

*The last stone of the row in the Glaze Brook Valley
has a hint of a cairn behind it*

The cairn above Harford Moor Gate

The cist

The cairn above Harford Moor Gate looks out over a wide expanse of the Erme's moorland landscape. It is situated about half a mile to the north of Harford Moor Gate where the cist sits in its cairn that still has seven stone of its retaining circle in situ. Two loose stones make up one end, but they are not original. Because of the missing end stone the length of the cist can not be ascertained. However, to give some idea of its length one side stone measures 40". Its width at one end measures 31", tapering to 24" at the other. Its lie is 58°NNW.

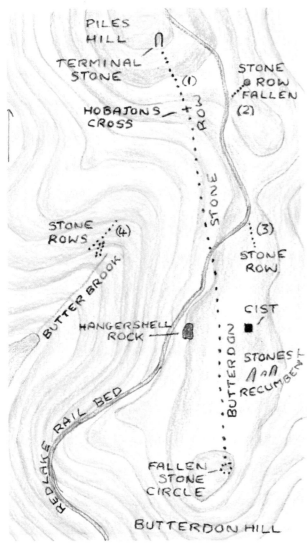

The granite pillar in the alignment

There are five stone rows, all of different lengths, between Piles Hill and Butterdon Hill. There is also one cist and several cairns both large and small to be found. After a short stroll along the old rail bed to the south the walker will spot on the right a standing stone on the peak of Piles Hill. This stone, re-erected a few years ago, is the terminal menhir of a row that runs along the moor from about a mile and a quarter away on Butterdon Hill. This monument is the second longest stone row on Dartmoor and in more recent history can be seen to have been conveniently utilised by the parishes of Harford and Ugborough as a section of their boundaries, they have even placed a few of their own granite pillars along the alignment. These can be identified by the scars of the feather and tare, such as the stone shown in the photograph above.

Hobajon's Cross

The terminal stone and boundary marker

There is also another stone that stands out from the rest; it is known as Hobajon's Cross, but whether this is an interloper or an original member of the row is open to conjecture. Before the menhir was discovered this stone was thought to be the termination of the row. Sadly there are any amount of stones missing or buried in the alignment and every member of the cairn circle at its outset have fallen some, like those in the row, now buried. Standing they would have been quite impressive.

A few stones of the row not far from the stone circle

The avenue near Spurrell's Cross

The sad sight of the fallen stone circle

The double row

The fallen stones of the alignment

To the east of the Hobajon's Cross on the other side of the old rail bed can be found an alignment where all the stones to be seen lie prostrate. They run away from a cairn that lies to its north-east. Whether the south-western end of this sad-looking monument ever reached the rail bed or was robbed by the railway would require excavation.

Also in a sad state is a stone avenue located near Spurrell's Cross (the refurbished cross with a replacement rugged head). This row, not very photogenic, begins its run from a cairn that has just two stones of its retaining circle remaining in place. There is evidence to be gathered while walking along its length that it could well have been a double row. The final stone of the seven still standing, situated just a few yards from the rail bed, stands just over knee high. With a little gentle pressing of one's booted feet, one can feel other stones beneath

the moorland vegetation that are no doubt other members of the alignment.

It is time the next monument to be discussed was placed on the Ordnance Survey maps. Running almost parallel with the Butter Brook is an intriguing couple of stone rows. Sadly not very distinguishable with the camera, I first came across these one day after deviating my walk back to Harford Moor Gate while a local farmer was out on the moor on his motorcycle rounding up his sheep. So as not to interfere with his work I strolled a little more south of my intended route. There is a double and a single row, the double row encroaches so close to the single row that they almost converge.

One could say that the two monuments, that are merely skeletons of their former selves, are related, and erected for some astrological purpose perhaps. Just a few of the single row stones show above the turf, while the tallest of the double stand within a foot or two from their line. Out of the two alignments it is only the shorter double row that has a related cairn from which it extends.

The single row

HANGERSHELL ROCK

The cist east of Hangershell Rock and (inset) the stones of the cist

Below and right: The fallen stones on Butterdon

Back up on the saddle of the moor east of Hangershell Rock can be found, with a little searching, the ruins of a cist. Since the photograph (above top) was taken, the moorland vegetation has grown and shrouded a great deal of this part of the saddle making it far more difficult for those interested to locate the remains of the monument. Two end stones and one side stone is all that can be viewed of the little grave; the cap stone like the cairn is nowhere to be seen. The length from end stone to end stone is 25", the width because of the absence of the miss-

ing side stone can not be ascertained. Its lie is 62°NNW.

A stroll further along the saddle towards the fallen stones of the cairn circle on Butterdon Hill, but keeping well to the east of its stone row, will bring the walker to two huge elongated stones lying on the ground. One is twenty-one feet in length the other merely three feet shorter.

There is another far smaller stone lying between them but whether it is related to the pair is a matter open to conjecture.

Cantrell stone row

Two great megaliths standing tall. Could this have been the scene on Butterdon Hill in prehistory?

Right on the very edge of the moor at Cantrell can be found another dilapidated stone row; it is in fact a double row with eleven stones to be counted in the southern more prominent line of the two (the tallest being 30"), with only six to be counted in the northern row, most barely showing above the turf. All run down the gentle slope from an associated cairn, sadly in the same condition as the rows. However, near the centre of the cairn is a large stone 40" long, but finishing in point 17" high, the wrong shape for it to be the side stone of a cist. I wonder, is it possible that the last stone of the southern row was actually the original final member? Now it sits damaged (with concrete preventing it from falling over) on the very edge of a bank created by those who built the rail track. William Crossing estimated the row to be 50 yards in length. Worth's tape made it 51 yards.

North of Cantrell lies Cuckoo Ball burial chamber. Now in ruins, this monument belonged to the Neolithic age. The stones that remain standing, like those that have been damaged and lie on the ground, sit in the ruins of the chamber's mound. To give some idea of the dimensions of the dolmen, the largest stone standing measures 5' 10" high, 3' 7" (the height compares to that of the Chun Quoit in Cornwall) wide. Its companion is 4'5" high by 7' 9" wide. The lie of the chamber is 12°ENE.

*   *   *

Cuckoo Ball dolmen looking to the west

Cuckoo Ball looking along the chamber to the south-west

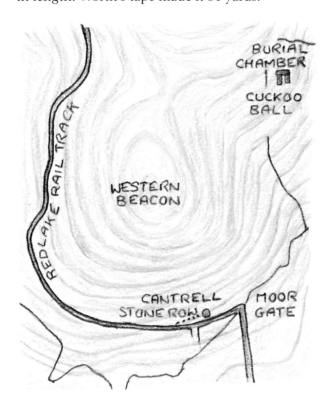

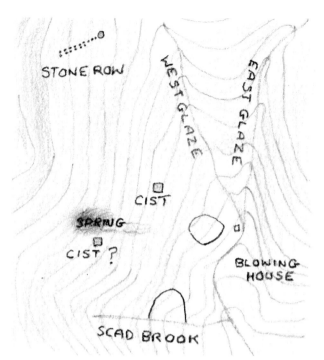

The view across the Scad Brook cist and (below) the stones of the cist

We are now in the Avon valley. The folk that constructed the enclosure that lies beside the left bank of the Scad Brook did so no doubt for the convenience of the water supply that ran along the bottom of their settlement. Still remaining in situ in the walls of one of the hut circles are its door jambs which can be seen in the photograph below.

Hut circle and door jambs

pletely buried can be seen as being of considerable length and, when standing, must have formed quite a monument. One imagines the climate must have been much drier when the row was erected, for today the ground at this spot is nearly always very wet, which could well be the reason that the stones fell down.

The view along the Avon Valley stone row and (inset) the last stone in the single row looking towards the double row

A few hundred yards to the north-west of the enclosure the walker will find, after some searching, the ruins of a cist. Sadly only one side stone and one end stone now remain. To give some idea of the size of the cist, the side stone can be measured at 49", while the end stone measures 16". Little of its cairn remains to be seen. The lie of the cist is 53°WNW.

A little further uphill to the north-west the walker will find a truly intriguing stone row. From its lower end it begins with a single line of stones from a cairn where all the material of its retaining circle has fallen. Those stones that are not com-

The Avon Valley double stone row

The single line of stones stretch for well over one hundred yards until reaching the double. From here the twins travel for another seventy yards or so till they come to a stop at what can only be described as the ghostly remains of another cairn. Whether measurements could be taken of this feature perhaps would rest on the possibility of an excavation. One can clearly see the remnants of a circle, especially on the north-west side of its circumference, one can also discern that the centre of this most interesting feature is concave.

Up on the saddle to the north-west, between the West Glaze and the East Glaze Brooks, is to be found the remarkable stone rows known as the Corringdon Ball alignments. Seven rows can be counted running from the north-west to the southeast. Somehow Samuel Rowe in his *A Perambulation of Dartmoor* counted eight. R.H. Worth in his count made it seven, but grouped them in two lines of three and one single line. None of the stones are of any great proportions. One row, that is the northeast and longest alignment, is for reasons known only to those that constructed it, isolated from the other six and runs from its own cairn. The six (or what may be two rows of three) run along the hillside from a stone circle measuring just over twelve yards in diameter, now containing only seven members in its circumference.

There can surely be no doubt that all seven of these rows have been robbed of many of their members for the construction of the nearby wall that borders the fields of Corringdon Ball Farm.

These photographs were taken many years before the last outbreak of Foot and Mouth disease rid the moor of extensive livestock grazing. Now a majority of the stones in these rows are hidden beneath a spread of moorland vegetation.

Above top: Stone rows running away from the stone circle
Above: Lines drawn showing the nine concentric circles

Below: The north-east alignment at Corringdon Ball

The East Glaze Brook double stone row

Less than a stone's throw from the outset of the rows, to the north-west, lie four cairns in close proximity. One in particular, measuring forty feet across, is fascinating in that it appears to contain nine stone circles. Whether it does or not, perhaps only excavation could prove one way or another.

* * *

Only a matter of yards away from the multiple alignments on Brent Fore Hill, on the other side of the East Glaze Brook, can be found a double stone row. First found in 1945 by a Mrs Watkin, it runs down the hill for near on one hundred and thirty six yards from its cairn. R.H. Worth tells us that in his day 42 stones were undoubtedly members of the row, twenty-seven of which were standing, with fifteen fallen. There are many spaces or stones miss-

ing in the alignment and two leats scythe their way through it, one dry, one still running water to Corringdon Ball Farm.

On the same hill close to the moorland gate of Corringdon Ball Farm, are the remains of a long barrow now in a most ruinous condition. The one stone to remain standing, has a height of 3' 9", and no doubt stands in its original position. Another huge stone, which appears to have been toppled but not totally prostrate, measures 11'10" long by 5' 10" in width to the ground. This stone's length would have at one time I am sure, been its height. The stone in the foreground of the photograph below, measuring 11' 2" by 7', I am sure was the feature's cap stone. The barrow is just over forty three yards in length. Its lie is 56°NW.

North of the Long Barrow, on Hickley Plain there are two stones that sit in the substantial remains of

Remains of the Long Barrow

The prostrate cap stone

The stone on Hickley Plain

a cairn. However, one stone stands on end appearing very much like that of a modern day headstone of a grave. It stands 36" high and 33" wide. It was most probably at one time a partner to the other stone, 32" long and with a lie of 3°NNE, lying a few inches away, which looks to have been turned on its end in more recent times. Its lie is north. No cap stone can be seen.

Another couple of stones, one completely buried in moorland vegetation, the other half covered, lie within the confines of a most ruinous cairn. The stones are believed to be those of a ruined cist. All lie more or less to the east of the last-mentioned ruin, just a few yards south-west of a running leat. One of the stones is an elongated specimen that appears just above the turf, it is 48" in length being long enough to be that of a side stone. Now com-

pletely shrouded, one end of the cist appears to be made up of two stones. However, a measurement of 20" inches on my tape cannot be trusted, for the exact end of the stone can not be precisely located. No cap stone can be seen. Their lie is 51°WNW and 62°WNW, respectively.

Below the aforementioned leat, sitting on the steepest slopes of Hickley Ridge, is another ruin to for the walker to view. Only two stones now survive in place, one side stone 48" long and one end stone measuring 21".

There is another stone that lies prostrate on the ground only inches away, half buried in moorland vegetation, that could well have been the complementary side stone of the cist. No cap stone can be found; also the mound of a cairn is non existent. The lie of the cist is 7°NNE.

A view over the ruinous cairn and (inset) the end stone of the cist

A view over the Hickley Ridge cist and (inset) the remaining stones of the cist

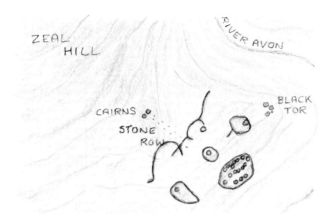

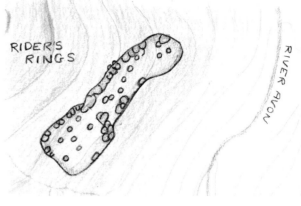

The partly hidden stones of the row at Black Tor
Inset: Possible end stone of the cist

The stone row at Black Tor above the Avon could easily be passed by those who are not aware of its presence. Only a few stones show above the turf. The double row runs from a cairn, one of two that sit alongside each other. Two of the more prominent stones, one from each row, can be seen in the photograph above just a few yards from their cairn that can be seen behind them.

Two stones that appear to be set within the confines of the same cairn could be those of what remains of a small cist.

*   *   *

The settlement of Riders Rings stretches across the side of Zeal Hill for (using the information gathered by William Crossing) 380 yards. Its circumference is 975 yards. The whole is made up of two enclosures, each with several hut circles and courts within their confines. It is best to visit this intriguing site during the winter months after the bracken has disappeared.

The site sits about 350' above the river Avon. It is no doubt South Dartmoor's equivalent to Grimspound, the prehistoric enclosure situated on the more northerly part of the moor. Yet nowhere near the same attention is paid to the Rings by the public, the reasons being no doubt that it far less accessible. There is no public highway running near it and no easy track. A steep climb is needed to reach the ridge before a walk of half a mile round the escarpment from Black Tor brings the stones of its impressive walls into view.

A view along the wall at Rider's Rings

This great feature is nigh on twice the size of its northern counterpart, with double the amount of hut circles and other ancillary buildings within its walls. The site includes a far more recent construction built utilising material from the prehistoric stone work, perhaps for use by a moorman caring for his livestock. This structure is 18' long and measure 9' at one end, and 7' at the other. There is also, if a walk along the northern walling is made, what appears to be two small compartments annexed to the outer walling.

One of the hut circles in the south enclosure

85

Top: Western Whittabarrow cairn. Eastern Whittabarrow can just been seen on the skyline.

Above: The ruined dwelling at Western Whittabarrow.

About a mile up hill to the north-west of the Rings can be found the impressive sight of Eastern Whittabarrow (White Barrow) cairn; Whytburghe as it was spelt in the days of the ancient perambulations of the forest. This huge pile of stones, 270′ in circumference, is topped by a rounded turret-shaped summit reminiscent of the huge Ballowall Barrow at St Just in West Cornwall. When the turret was erected no one seems to know; however, one can surmise that it must have been in the early years of the twentieth century for it was not written about by William Crossing in his guide to Dartmoor, first published in 1909, but it was there when I began trekking the moor in the early 1970s. On a clear day the cairn can be seen from all quarters of the moor and certain areas of the in-country.

If Eastern Whittaburrow has been disfigured, its partner of Western Whittaburrow, standing on the same hillside about a three-quarters of a mile away to the north-west, has been seriously mutilated. This was done by the men employed on the naphtha works at Shipley Bridge. They helped themselves and reworked the stones of the cairn to con

struct the dwelling, the ruins of which still stand to a considerable height. The cairn was also employed as a Forest boundary delineating the extent of the royal hunting ground after it was transferred here from Eastern Whittabarrow. It was also used as a boundary when Sir William Petre placed one of his crosses on top of the cairn. With its arm and head knocked off, the cross is now wedged crudely upside down among the sad remains of the cairn.

A steep climb up on to the escarpment to the South of Huntingdon clapper will find the remains of a cairn circle. I am sure there are more or were more stones (some buried or perhaps robbed for one reason or another) involved with this monument, however only eleven stones of the outer circle and three of an the inner could be seen when I counted them. Compared to the rest of the stones, two members of the outer circle that have fallen are much larger. The diameter of the cairn taken from the outer extremities of two standing stones and taken from north-west to south-east is 36' 6". The granite of three of the stones contains quartz crystals, one with a finer display than the other two.

Owing to the height and density of the moorland vegetation the whole of the monument cannot be photographed. The top right hand photograph shows one member of the inner circle and two of the outer circle.

The photograph (opposite right) displays members of both circles and in the background can be seen two of the larger enclosures that can be found on the slopes of Huntingdon Warren. Also on the warren can be seen the huge dilapidated pile of the Heap of Sinners cairn, shown below.

Members stones of both circles at Huntingdon

Stones of the inner and outer circles

*   *   *

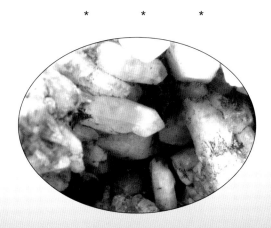

Quartz crystals appear on three of the stones

Below: The Heap of Sinners cairn

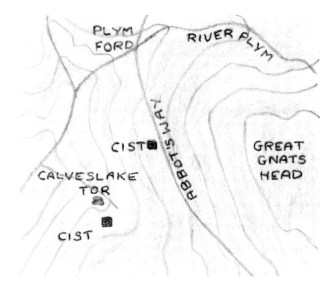

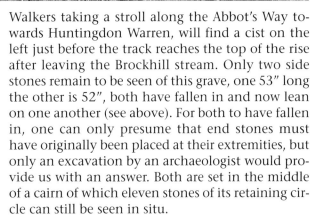

Walkers taking a stroll along the Abbot's Way towards Huntingdon Warren, will find a cist on the left just before the track reaches the top of the rise after leaving the Brockhill stream. Only two side stones remain to be seen of this grave, one 53" long the other is 52", both have fallen in and now lean on one another (see above). For both to have fallen in, one can only presume that end stones must have originally been placed at their extremities, but only an excavation by an archaeologist would provide us with an answer. Both are set in the middle of a cairn of which eleven stones of its retaining circle can still be seen in situ.

*   *   *

Near the head of the River Harbourne can be spotted a standing stone (opposite). It is the only menhir on the southern moor that is isolated from any other known prehistoric remains. It stands just over eight feet high, and leans towards the river to the west. About a third of the way up its length can be seen, cut into its narrowest side, a bench mark.

*   *   *

Between Shipley Tor and the lower northern slopes of Holne Moor there are nearly three dozen cairns; none holds particular interest except for the mound of stones that might have at one time buried the rock pile of Middle Pupers Tor.

Most of the stones, except those placed in a pile by the visitors, are scattered around the immediate vicinity, but many I suspect have been robbed for wall building. There is associated with the little tor two great un-cut orthostatic stones that seem to be set in position. One measures 3' 3" high by 3' 9" with a thickness of 10", its companion standing beside it has the dimensions of 3' 4" by 3' 8" with a thickness of 8". What these stones are here for I do not know. On my first visit many years ago I thought they might belong to the same period as the cairn; now I have my doubts, for there are three similar shaped stones standing among the rock pile of Outer Pupers, and on the edge of one of these can be seen the tell-tale marks of feather and tare. These can be seen on the stone in the centre of the lower photograph.

About half a mile further along the ridge to the north-west on the highest point of southern Dartmoor, three more cairns can be viewed. On the perimeter of the largest can be seen the vestige of its retaining circle.

On Rider's Hill can be found a cairn that has been robbed almost out of existence, although three stones of different shapes can be seen to occupy a little of the cairn's ground space.

Above: Outer Pupers Tor

Below: The cut stone – evidence of feather and tare

Middle Pupers Tor

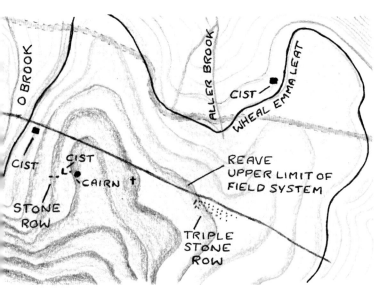

The fallen stone and the distant reave

We are now in the River Dart Watershed. The first cist to be found on the lower slopes of Holne Moor lies a couple of hundred yards to the right of the Aller Brook between the two leats that run along the hillside. Its approximate internal measurements are 42" long on one side and 36" on the other; it is 21" wide. There is no sign of its cap stone or the mound of its cairn, however, there are a couple of stones protruding through the turf that could well be the remains of its retaining circle. The lie of the cist is 56°NNW.

There is a triple stone row to be found on Holne Moor, it lies to the south of a boundary reave that runs along the hillside. Many stones could be seen when I first visited the monument but now sadly only a few appear above the vegetation. Compared to the stones that begin the alignments the stones along the triple row are comparatively small. Only one stands in place, with the tallest now lying prostrate. It is 11′ 6″ long. The reave, dating from prehistoric times, can be seen running along towards the centre of the picture above.

Holne Moor cairn formerly had a stone row

Cist on the lower slopes of Holne Moor and (below) the stones of the cist

Farther along the hillside, still to the south of the reave, the walker will pass a cross (Horn's Cross), and a little farther on, the eye will catch sight of a couple of cairns. However, the cairn of most interest appears as a mound shrouded in bracken looking down the hill towards the O Brook. This cairn at one time had a stone row running down the hill away from it; now sadly only two stones survive of the monument. On the right of the row can be seen another two stones; the longer of the two I think is the side stone of a cist, the shorter stone I am sure is its end stone. The pair are 45" in length and 24" respectively. Its lie, like most cists on the moor, is within the mean direction north-west–south-east, at 1°NNE.

Holne Moor, the second cairn and (inset) Holne Ridge higher cist

It is thought that these pair of stones are like the two to the left of them, the remains of a double stone row leading away from the cairn that lies up hill to the east.

Farther downhill to the north-west the walker will find another monument, a stone of large proportions standing on edge making up one side of a cist. The remainder of the cist lies 2' 6" below the top of the boulder which is 5' 3" long. Each end of the cist appears to be made up of two stones with just one forming the other side. The width at one end measures 35", the other 29". However, owing to one end stone leaning inwards, its length cannot be easily ascertained. A stone that looks as if it has been broken, resting on the outer confines of the cist, could well be a section of the cap stone. All lies within the considerable remains of its cairn. Its lie is 2°NNE.

*   *   *

The large side stone of the cist and (inset) the remains of the cist with what may be a broken cap stone

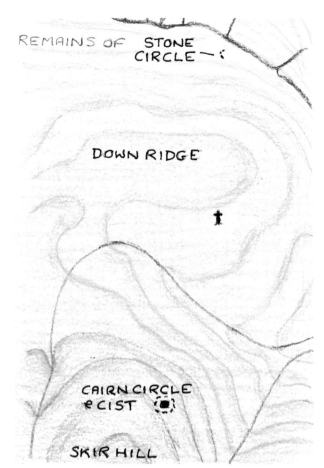

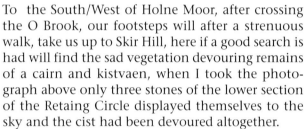

Above: Skir Hill cairn and cist.

Below: The set stone south-east of the Skir Hill circle.

To the South/West of Holne Moor, after crossing the O Brook, our footsteps will after a strenuous walk, take us up to Skir Hill, here if a good search is had will find the sad vegetation devouring remains of a cairn and kistvaen, when I took the photograph above only three stones of the lower section of the Retaing Circle displayed themselves to the sky and the cist had been devoured altogether.

Below Skir Hill and through the old disused tin works, up the hill and passed Down Ridge Cross and the remains of a stone circle will be seen. Only four stone now survive standing with two lying almost prostrate. One can only surmise that the sad demise of this Circle that looks out over a great deal of the northern moor, is owing to the New Take Wall to the North. Not to many yards South/East of the Circle is a set stone standing alone whether there is a relationship between it and the Circle only those who may have placed it there, will ever know.

Down Ridge circle.

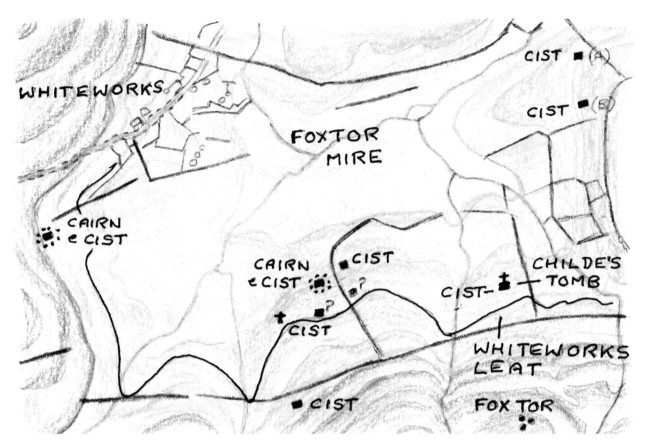

To reach our next group of antiquities from Down Ridge, we can cross the stream of Deep Swincombe and follow the lower contours of Ter Hill keeping well above the Wheel Emma Leat untill we meet a gate in the new take wall of Foxtor Farm. However, the going can be quite heavy in places. here not far west of the gate can be located a cist that sits in the remains of its cairn. The Grave itself except for one end stone that leans slightly inwards is in fairly good condition. However because of its frailties, the true length of its sides can not be ascertaind, but the width can and measures 26" at one end tapering to 21" at the other. Its cap stone leans on one corner of the Grave. The cists lie is 52WNW.

View across the cist west of Foxtor Farm gate and (inset) the cap stone.

93

The second cist in the Foxtor Farm fields

The stones of the cist in Foxtor Farm fields

To the south of the last-mentioned cist, still within the fields of Foxtor Farm can be found another. It is in nowhere near such good condition. In fact only one end and one side stone remain in position; the other side stone as fallen and the other end stone, like the cap stone, is sadly missing altogether. The whole stands in just a faint remnant of its cairn. To give some idea of the size of the cist, the length of the side stone is 51" and the one end stone measures 24". Its lie is 53°WNW. Reed is fast encroaching on both little monuments.

From the last mentioned cist, Childe's Tomb can be seen across the infant Swincombe River to the south-south-west. The cross that sits in its socket stone on the great elongated blocks of granite have nothing to do with the grave below it. Without going into the legend to deeply, Childe was a hunting landowner who froze to death out here in this valley. The cist below the cross and its plinth has both its side stones and its end stones in place. The internal length of the cist is 61", its width, such of it that can be measured, is 2". Its lie is 55°NW. The kerb circle that surrounds the whole is a poor example of a reconstruction.

A pair of stones to be found to the west of Childe's Tomb, beside the top end of an old tinners' gully has not previously been mentioned by other writers or experts in the field. It may or not be the remains of a cist but I think it is at least worth recording here. It sits on a rise in the surrounding ground, and to give some idea of its size, the length of the side stone is 60", and the end stone measures 27". Its lie is 8°NE.

Childe's Tomb and (inset) the cist.

94

FOXTOR MIRE

Possible remains of a cist west of Childe's Tomb and (inset) the side stone.

The stones of this cist are not easily located

One the best examples of a cist on Dartmoor

Not one of the easiest cists to locate sits lower down the hillside from the cist last mentioned. It consist of two ends and a side stone, which itself is made up of two stones. To give some idea of its internal dimensions the length from end stone to end stone is 39" and 42" respectively. No cap stone can be found nor any sign of a cairn. Its lie is 55°WNW.

Although it cannot be seen from the last mentioned cist one of the best examples to be found on the moor can be viewed on the west side of the tinners' gully. The photograph above was taken before the last outbreak of foot and mouth disease, while the two photos on the following page, were taken a few years after. The cist has all four stones in place. Its internal dimensions are 28" long by 18"wide. Its lie is 51°WNW. Its cairn circle is in fact oval in shape consisting of seven stones, with perhaps one missing. The cap stone is also missing.

The cist and (inset) its stones photographed after the foot and mouth outbreak of 2001

An object of intrigue, the granite slab 44" in length

The second stone

To the south-west on the slightly higher ground, just a couple of yards from the old Whiteworks leat, can be found an intriguing artefact. A hole in the ground a couple of feet deep, unlike that of a tinners' trial pit, it is four feet wide and seven feet six inches long. The ground above it is raised like that of a cairn. Inside the elongated hole running along one side it, can be seen a stone slab 44" long by 24" high, pictured above. Another stone three feet six inches away, standing at right angles to it, measures 27" wide by 25" high. These two stones could well be the remains of a cist, but how they became separated can only be speculated upon and doubts are raised by that fact that all the cists in the vicinity of the mire lie between 55° and 51° while the slab which could pass as a side stone, points to the north.

Another cist can be found to the south of Goldsmith's Cross. It lies on the infant slopes of Crane Hill, on the higher side of the Foxtor Newtake wall. The feature can be seen showing just above the turf, but it is in quite a sad state of preservation with only one side stone, consisting of two stones, and both ends stones remaining. The internal length of the one side is 48"; the two end stones measure 34" and 26" respectively. There is no sign of its cap stone, no doubt robbed for the convenience of the stone walling nearby. Its lie is 54°WNW.

A view over the cist on the lower slopes of Crane Hill with Foxtor Newtake wall in the middle distance. Inset: The stones of the cist

Above: View over the cairn beside the Devonport Leat

Below: The stones of the cist

Overlooking the great mire is the Devonport Leat and sitting beside this watercourse is a substantial cairn with a beautiful cist in its midst. The cairn and its retaining circle have not escaped the hand of modern man, for although the running leat is well above it, the original course chosen for the water to flow cut across the western sides of its perimeter. However, thirteen large stones standing and one that is lying prostrate can still be counted in its circumference. The cist is very neat in its construction with both side stones measuring 34" in length, while the end stones are both 24". Its lie is 53°WNW.

*   *   *

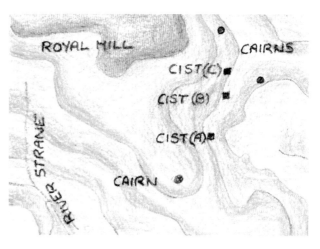

Royal Hill lies to the north of Foxtor Mire and here on its lower slopes can be found three cists. The first cist (A) has one side stone in place measuring 55", this is locked at one end behind an end stone 23" long. At the other end three stones appear to make up the extremity; there is an elongated stone half buried to one side of the cist that could well

Royal Hill cist A

Close up of Royal Hill cist A

Royal Hill cist B

Close up of Royal Hill cist B

Royal Hill cist C – before foot and mouth outbreak of 2001

Close up of Royal Hill cist C – a more recent photo

have been the missing side stone. The lie of the cist is 51°WNW. Fourteen small and large stones make up its circle. No cap stone can be located.

Just a couple of hundred yards away to the north-north-East is cist (B). Time has ravaged its cairn with only three or four stones of its retaining circle to be counted. The cist is almost square and to give some idea of its size, the sides are 31" and 38", the end stones are 29" and 35". Its lie is 56°NW. No cap stone can be seen. It is a shame, but the last time I saw this monument the moorland grass was absolutely smothering it.

The smallest of the three monuments in the row of cairns can be seen about a hundred yards away, but for how much longer is anyone's guess, for reed and grass is beginning to cover it (compare the two photos above). One side of the cist is inclining towards the other, the consequence of missing one end stone, the other leaning inwards. Owing to the side stones being partially covered no idea can be given of its size.

There are nine stones of the retaining circle still standing proud above the turf. Its lie is 52°WNW. The cap stone is missing.

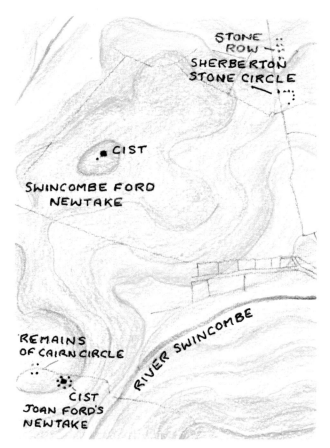

Top: The view over the cist north of Joan Ford's Newtake

Above: The tumbled stones of the cist

The next site of interest lies about two-thirds of a mile away to the east-south-east in the field of Joan Ford's Newtake. Here a cist sits close to the wall a few yards to the left of the field gate. It is complete and in good condition bar one of its side stones having fallen inwards. The cist, with its cap stone propped against one end, measures 42" on one side and just over that on the other. One end stone is 26" in length while its opposite number is shorter at 20". Those building the field wall robbed its cairn circle of its northern extremity, however, sixteen stones still remain more or less in place. The lie of the cist is 54°WNW.

To the north of Joan Ford's Newtake, near the top of the Swincombe Ford Newtake, can be found a cist in the most ruinous state. Today its stones are tumbled and broken, while its cap stone lies cum-bersomely in the centre of it. Only a faint remains of its covering cairn are visible, with one slab of granite standing upright a couple of yards away to the south-west. The lie of the cist, because of its ru-inous condition, cannot be taken.

East of the ruined cist and a few yards farther still, east of a reave, can be located a double stone row. When I say locate, it is certainly no spectacular site to be seen from miles away, for not one stone shows but an inch above the turf. When I viewed it only seven in the eastern alignment could be photographed as being members of a continuous line. The photographs overleaf show them as they approach the top of the rise.

The view over Joan Ford's Newtake cist and (inset) the stones of the cist

The stones of Sherberton Double stone row in order as they ascend the hill

D

A

E

B

F

C

G

SHERBERTON STONE CIRCLE

Sherberton stone circle

The large boulder that may be part of the circle

The view across the Crock of Gold cist and (below) the stones of the cist

As the top of the rise is approached members of a stone circle can be seen. Unlike the stone row these protrude well above the ground, but only ten members have survived the test of time since. There are two lying prostrate and whether the large slim boulder sitting at an angle among the stone of a reave, is a member of the circle is open to conjecture. The situation reminds me of that of the circle entangled with Willingswalls Reave in the River Plym area.

On the north side of Royal Hill can be found the cist named the Crock of Gold. It sits beside the Princetown to Hexworthy track. This grave is a very neat specimen with all stones in place. Its internal dimensions are 32" along one side and 30" on the other; its width at one end is 20" tapering to 16" at the other. Its lie is 56°NW. Its cap stone rests in the west side of the cairn, of which five stones of its retaining circle are still in place.

A couple of hundred yards uphill to the south of the last mentioned monument, not far from a huge tinners' delving, walkers will find the scant remains of another cairn and cist (D on the map left). There is nothing special about it, in fact it barely shows above the ground one end stone is missing its length can not be ascertained, however its width can, which is 24" at one end and 22" at the other. Its lie is 54°WNW.

Blakey Tor Cist B

To the South of Blakey Tor, is a cist (B on the map left) in very good condition. All four of its stones are more or less still in the position they were when they were first placed here. To give some idea of its size the internal dimensions is 37" along one side and 35" along the other. The width is 20" at one end and 19" at the other. Its lie is 59°NNW. Its cap stone rests on one corner of the grave. It is a shame that its cairn does not appear today in the same good shape.

Royal Tor Cist D

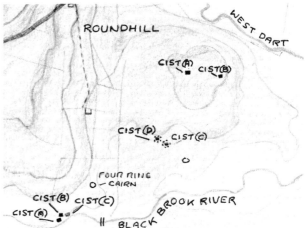

A small cemetery of three cists can be found nestling beside the Black Brook, one cist (A on the map above) is the more complete of the three with all its stones intact. However, the end stone nearest the brook as fallen outward. Estimating where the stone would have originally rested, the internal length of one side would have been 55" and the other 53"; its width is 29" tapering to 27". Its lie is 58°NNW. Its huge cap stone, as the photograph below shows, rests on the west side of the cist.

Below: Cist A lying beside the Black Brook and (inset) the stones of the cist with the cap stone resting against them

Top: The view over Blakey Tor Cist (A) and (above) the stones of the cist

A hundred yards or so to the West of the last cist is another (A on the map previous page). This grave is not in such a good state of preservation, for sadly it has one end stone missing, the cap stone as been placed to one side, close to one end. Lacking one end stone its length cannot be accurately measured, however its width is 21" across at one end tapering to 17" at the other. Its lie is 56°NW.

*View over Blackbrook cist B and
(inset) the stones of the cist*

Cist (B) can be found just a few yards away but a little farther from the brook. It is in nowhere near such good condition as the last mentioned cist. Only one side stone remains in place, while its opposite number has fallen outward.

The northern end stone still holds its original position, while its opposite number has been moved and now lies askew near the southern extremity of the ruin. Its lie is 58°NNW. There is no cap stone to be found, also, like cist (A), there is little sign of a cairn.

Cist (C), below and inset right, is the last of the three resting beside the Black Brook to be recorded in this survey. It is quite beautiful, a piece of prehistoric 'art' that would hardly be out of place in any modern gallery. Both side stones along with

both end stones have survived in place. Its internal dimensions are 39″ long on one side and 37″ on the other; its width is 32″ at one end tapering to 28″ at the other. Its lie is 59°NNW. However, with all its attractive appearance, its cap stone is missing, and there is little sign of its cairn. There are however three or four stones that seem to be set in the ground that run away from the western side stone.

*   *   *

View over the cist on the western edge of Round Hill and (inset) the stones of the cist

On the eastern edge of Round Hill will be found another cist. This grave has all its component parts there for the walker to see and looks down on a settlement of twenty or so hut circles nestled in the confluence of the West Dart and the Black Brook where those interred no doubt once resided. The internal dimensions of this almost perfect specimen are 37" along one side and 35" on the other. Its width is 22" at one end and 21" at the other. Its cap stone has been left resting on its eastern end where the grave robbers left it. The lie of the cist is 53°WNW. Only thing is missing from the scene, the cairn.

Half a mile or so away as the crow flies to the northeast, high on the eminence that is Round Hill can be found, on the western edge of the summit, a cist. It comprises two side stones and only one end stone; the displaced end stone could well be the slab that lies recumbent near the western corner of the cist. If the displaced end stone originally sat across the ends of the side stones the internal length of the cist would have been 51" at one side and 49" at the other. The width at one end is 26" tapering to 22" at the other. Its cap stone, as the photograph above displays, sits on one of the side stones. Its lie is 52°WNW. All sits in the remains of its cairn, of which at least one stone of its retaining circle can be seen.

View over the cist on the eastern edge of Round Hill and (inset) the stones of the cist

Above: The first cairn on the southern side of Round Hill and (inset) the stones of the cist

There are two other cists in the vicinity of Round Hill; these lie below its southern slopes. Unlike the two up on the summit, this pair have not survived the test of time. Of the first, it appears that only one side stone and one end stone now remain in place, however I would not dismiss altogether the purpose of another stone that is half buried by the surrounding turf. To give some idea of the size of the cist, the length of the one side stone is 32" and the width from it to the partially buried stone is 23", which is an average width of cists across the moor. Another flat stone, lying on one side of the much depleted cairn, could well be the grave's cap stone. The lie of the cist is 53°WNW.

Just a couple of yards away, on slightly higher ground, is the other ruinous cist. One longer stone lying here, suggesting the side of a cist, is partially buried by the cairn's recently-formed turf and cannot be measured to its full extent. The measurement that can be taken reveals the stone to be 24" in length, but whether a stone, which runs more or less parallel to it 18" away is its opposite number, only an excavation could tell. The lie of the cist is 53°WNW.

*   *   *

Below left: The second cairn on the southern side of Round Hill and (below) the stones of the cist

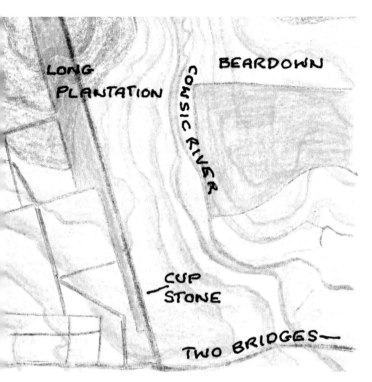

Location of the Long Plantation cup stone

The Long Plantation cup stone

A cup stone can be found built into the wall that runs alongside the road by Long Plantation. It can be spotted if walking from the main Tavistock to Two Bridges road to Holming Beam. Exactly how many depressions there are on the stone is hard to tell; if one wishes sixteen can be counted, however, six of varying sizes can be seen for sure, with two more oblong in shape than round. Why someone had to paint the numbers on it, beggars belief.

Conies Down lies just over two miles to the north of the cup stone. Running down the slope of the Down is a double stone row. As with all rows, the stones here vary in size, while those in the lower end of the row are small with some barely showing above the turf. At the higher end the stones are much larger. When I made a survey of the row, I counted twenty-one stones running down the left side and twenty down the right. Altogether there were eleven pairs that stand side by side. There are eighteen missing or buried. The row, according to past antiquarians varied in length, from Samuel Rowe's 529', William Crossing's 350' to Robert Burnard's 588'. When I put my tape measure to it I made it 554'.

Conies Down Double stone row and (inset) Beardown and Conies Down monuments map

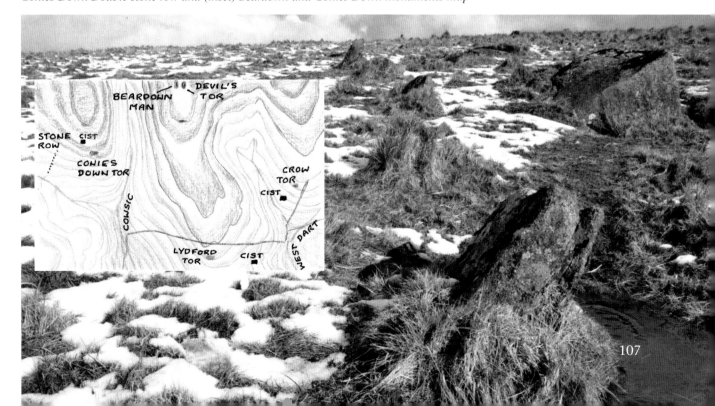

107

The view across Conies Down cist and (inset) the stones of the cist

High above the double row to the north-west can be found the second highest situated cist on Dartmoor. It is sited unusually near the edge of its burial cairn rather than in its centre. The state of the cairn gives one the idea that it has been delved into but, with that said, it appears that there was never a central cist. Only three stones of this oddly shaped grave remain in place today. The longest, more substantial stone, with a lie of 57°NNW I have taken to be its side stone, and to give some idea of the cist's size that stone is 57" long. The two remaining side stones are 34" and 54" respectively.

Across the Cowsic River stands Beardown Man the most isolated menhir on Dartmoor. It stands there with its height a few inches above eleven feet, close to the rock pile of Devil's Tor having had all the elements thrown at it since Bronze Age man placed it there. The photographs opposite display two sides of the fascinating feature.

The view across Beardown cist and (inset) the stones of the cist

East of Lydford Tor, close by some tinners' workings, can found a cist. Although not in a very good condition, all its component stones are there to see. One end stone is leaning, while its opposite number is hidden beneath moorland turf. While one side stone is still firmly in place the other is leaning inward. Owing to the fragile state of the one side, the width of the cist can not be truly ascertained. However to give some idea of its size, there is a measurement of nearly 48" from one end to the other. A slab half buried on top of the cairn could well be the cap stone. A couple of stones of the cairn's retaining circle still survive. The lie of the cist is 62°NNW.

The cist to be found on the lower south-west slope of Crow Tor does not appear on the Ordnance Survey 1:25000 Outdoor Leisure map. Both of its side stones and both end stones remain in their set

positions; one side stone can be excused for leaning slightly inwards for it has the weight of the cap stone leaning against it. The internal dimensions of the cist are 33" at both ends, while the sides differ dramatically from 43" down to 28". Its lie is 52°WNW. A great deal of the higher portion of its cairn is still intact with a few stones of its retaining circle still in place. In comparison, the lower portion has almost vanished altogether.

* * *

The view across Crow Tor cist and (inset) the stones of the cist

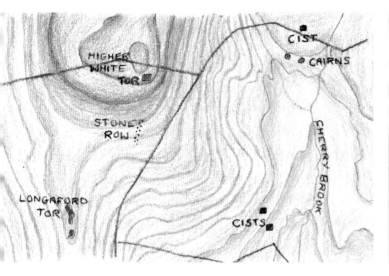

Higher White Hill stone row

The stone row on the slope between Higher White Tor and the conical rock pile of Longaford Tor is in fact a double row. Very few stones now remain, no doubt robbed for the nearby newtake wall. No more than a dozen stones now stand in place. Some can be seen to have fallen and others have over the years been buried beneath the moorland vegetation. Whether this monument has been ruined by modern man, or was never completed is virtually impossible to know for there seems to be no beginning or end to the structure, no cairn or blocking stone like those associated with other alignments.

The general awareness of the ruin at Crockern Tor (below), so I am led to believe, is due to Dr Tom Greeves. It sits in the rough moorland landscape among a fair acreage of stones and boulders. Only one member of a cist, which appears to be a side stone, survives today along with a small portion of its cairn. This stone is 48" long, and its lie is 48°W.

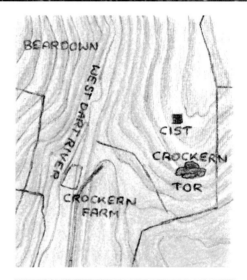

*   *   *

The view over Crockern Tor cist and (inset) the side stone of the cist

Left and below: The higher Cherrybrook cist

West of the Cherry Brook on the rock- and boulder-strewn slopes of Stennen Hill can be located a cist in almost perfect condition, bar the great slab of its cap stone that has been moved over to rest on the cist's downhill side. The internal measurements are 45″ on one side and 43″ on the other. Its width is 27″ at one end and 26″ at the other. All sits more or less in the centre of its cairn which has a few of stones of its retaining circle showing through the turf. The lie of the cist differs from most on the moor, in that its direction is 2°NNE.

A little further downhill in an east-west direction from the last-mentioned monument will be found another cist. However this specimen has not survived the test of time so well. Only one side stone can now be seen, with most of it shrouded in moorland vegetation. To give some idea of the size of the cist, the length of the one stone that leans inward can be measured at 52″. Measuring from this stone to where its opposite number would have been is 38″. Only four stones of its retaining circle remain to show above the turf. The lie of the cist is 54°WNW.

Below and right: The lower Cherrybrook cist

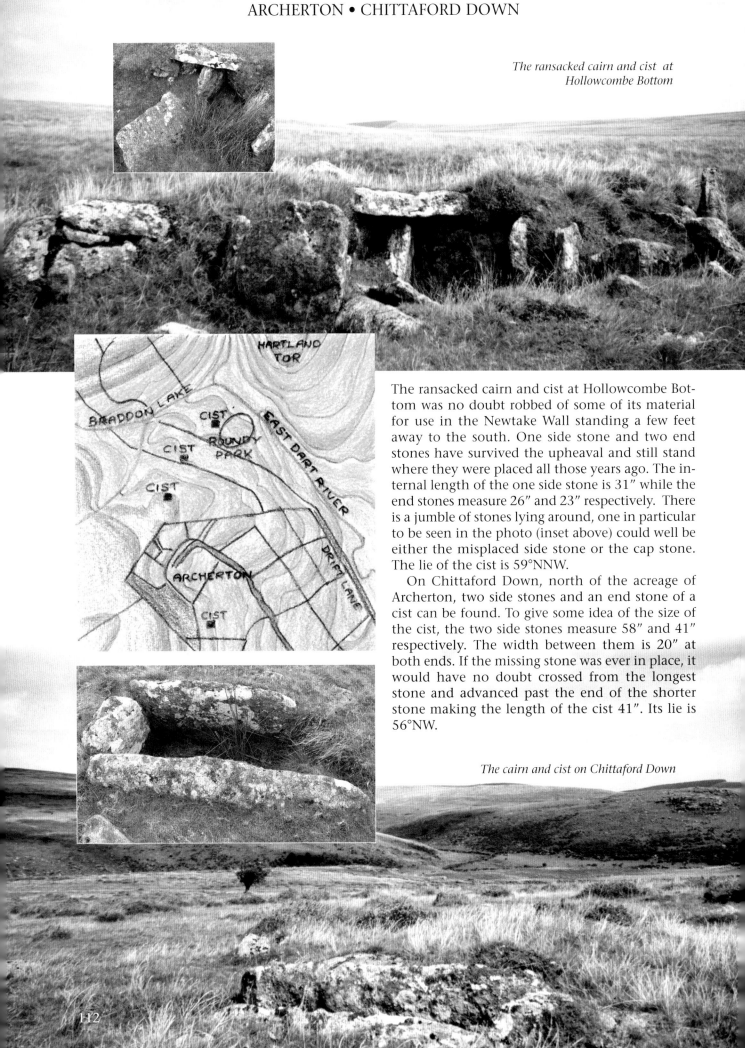

The ransacked cairn and cist at Hollowcombe Bottom

The ransacked cairn and cist at Hollowcombe Bottom was no doubt robbed of some of its material for use in the Newtake Wall standing a few feet away to the south. One side stone and two end stones have survived the upheaval and still stand where they were placed all those years ago. The internal length of the one side stone is 31" while the end stones measure 26" and 23" respectively. There is a jumble of stones lying around, one in particular to be seen in the photo (inset above) could well be either the misplaced side stone or the cap stone. The lie of the cist is 59°NNW.

On Chittaford Down, north of the acreage of Archerton, two side stones and an end stone of a cist can be found. To give some idea of the size of the cist, the two side stones measure 58" and 41" respectively. The width between them is 20" at both ends. If the missing stone was ever in place, it would have no doubt crossed from the longest stone and advanced past the end of the shorter stone making the length of the cist 41". Its lie is 56°NW.

The cairn and cist on Chittaford Down

The remains of the north-east cairn and (inset) the stones of the cist

The cist that lies to the north-east of the last mentioned, was new to me, until my wife came across it in the summer of 2008. It sits in the remains of its cairn which is rapidly being swallowed up by the fast encroaching reeds.

As the photograph above shows one of the cist's side stones is missing. None of the remaining stones touch another and because of this the cist's dimensions cannot be ascertained. However to give some idea of it size, the one side stone measures 33" while the two side stones are 24" and 20" long respectively. The width between the two stones is 24". Its lie is 57°WNW.

This cist that lies beside the north-western wall of Roundy Park is a restoration. It is one of the largest on the moor with one side being made up of two stones. The approximate internal measurements of this side is 75" while its opposite number is a lot shorter at 60". The ends measure 48" and 47" respectively. Two large slabs of granite are employed as the cap stone.

When antiquarian Robert Burnard first came across it both end stones were still in their original positions, including three side stones. Two side stones lay prostrate on the ground, one of them was found lying within the confines of the cist, while the other lay outside. The two cover stones (cap stones) were found lying away from one another, one of which had fallen into the cist. Its partner had been thrown down the slight slope a short distance from the cist. Before the restoration took place the interior of the cist was delved out and sifted, the effort being rewarded with finds of two fragments of flint, and some charcoal that turned out to be that of bone. It appears that twelve stones make up the retaining circle. Its lie is 4°NNE.

The cist at the north-west wall of Roundy Park

The cist sits in private ground and permission is necessary if you wish to enter. The cist is complete except for clear evidence of a cap stone. When the grave was excavated by Robert Burnard in the nineteenth century he found it to be paved. The internal dimensions are 38″ along one side and 37″ along the other. The end stones measures 34″ and 33″ respectively. Its lie is 60°NNW. Eight stones can be counted of its retaining circle, some still set in their place in the ground.

Above: The cist and the stones of its retaining circle lie in private ground. Inset: The stones of the cist

Below: Lake Head Hill cairn Circle

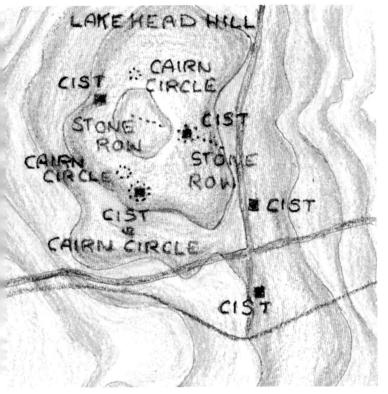

South of Archerton can be seen the fascinating prehistoric remains on the hill of Lake Head. This hill must have been highly revered by the people of the time for it is littered with their grave sites. Besides an enclosure named Kraps Ring, which is met with as one ascends the hill, lies a cairn circle with thirteen stones still showing well above the turf, some are touching one another like that of a kerb circle, others have spaces between them where the stones have been lost or are buried beneath the soil.

The cist that once lay in the conifer forest.

The stones of the cist with the cap stone missing.

This neat little cist (above) lies now out in the open among the stumps of the fir trees that only a few years ago shrouded the area. It can be found a couple of hundred yards to the south-west of the Lake Head cairn circle. Its internal dimensions are 36" on boths sides, although one of the side stones is split. The length of its ends are 20" and 22" respectively. Its lie is 55°WNW.

Since the top photograph was taken the cist has filled with forest debris and vegetation. There is no cap stone or cairn, the stones carted away no doubt for employment elsewhere.

The stone row (below) lies almost on the summit of the hill that run east to west. Worth suggested this row originally had its beginnings at the cist previously mentioned. However, I can't see this to be so, for a stone that appears to be a blocking stone halts the row a great many yards short of the cist, indicating that the row began its travel on the west of the hill. Only a dozen stones now survive.

The cairn and cist to the south-east of Lakehead Hill and (below) viewed from the opposite direction

To the south-east of the last mentioned alignment can be found another consisting of eleven stones leading away from a cairn circle and cist. There is controversy attached to this monument in respect of the cist and the stones of the row. R. H. Worth in the book *Worth's Dartmoor* casts doubt the construction of its restoration in 1895, saying the "kist-vaen is outsize for the stones comprised". Also the stone row starts from within the circle unlike that of any other on Dartmoor. The circle consist of six stones. The internal measurements of the cist are 62" along one side and 52" on the other. Its end stones measure 46" and 42" respectively. Its lie is 55°WWN.

The Lakehead cairn Circle comprising ten stones

South-west of the previous monument, a cairn circle lies on open ground with ten stones making up its circumference. The spaces between the stones, being so irregular in distance, suggest that the ten we see today are fewer in number than those originally completing the circle. Its diameter is 22′ 5″.

Just a glance to the south-east and the visitor to the site will notice another circle of stones, again with ten stones making up the ring. Here again there are enough empty spaces between the member stones for another six or seven stones to have been included. An added feature with this circle is the cist in its centre; sadly only one side stone and two end stones can be seen and felt beneath its great cap stone. To give some idea of its size, the one side stone measures 44″, while the two end stones are 23″ and 21″ respectively. Its lie is 52°WWN.

This Lakehead cairn circle also has ten stones but includes a central cist

leans slightly inward, and has been mutilated by a sledgehammer leaving at least half of it missing, but for the part that remains buried in the ground. From this surviving portion its length can be ascertained at 64″. The lie of the stones is 59°WNW. All sit within the great spread of its cairn, with only one stone of its retaining circle to be seen today.

This cist (below) lies a few hundred yards along the track to the south and, like the last mentioned, was hidden by the same forest canopy. This specimen has two side stones still in position with a trig stone supporting the northern one. One end stone can be seen. While beneath the canopy very little vegetation grew to obscure the stones but now, out in the open, vegetation is gradually encroaching on the cist, getting ready to devour it. The length of the side stones from the end stone is 47″ and 44″ respectively; the width from one side to the other is 31″. The monument's lie is 60°WNW. Very little of its cairn now survives.

The ruined cist

This sad ruin (above) can be found to the east of the last mentioned site, on the eastern side of the track that runs south-to-north over the hill. Not so very long ago it was hidden beneath a canopy of evergreen branches. Only two side stones have survived into the present day. The more prominent stone, that still stands upright as if being to large for use elsewhere, is 63″ long. Its opposite number

Below: The cist lying alongside the track to the south with (inset) the stones of the cist now covered by vegetation

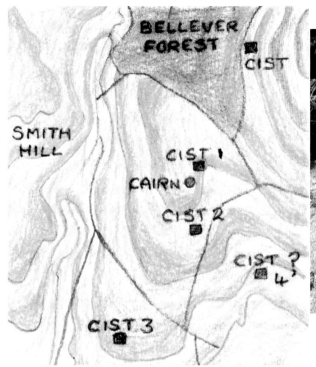

This cist can be found tucked in beside the conifers of Bellever Forest with Bellever Tor overlooking all. The grave consists of one end stone, and two side stones that measure 53″ and 48″ respectively. If the missing end stone was ever in place and it crossed from the longest side stone to the end of the shortest, the length of the cist would be 48″. Its width at one end is 27″ tappering to 20″ at the other. Its lie is 58°NNW. The ample weight of its cap stone sits on the cist's northern side, leaving all sitting in the midst of its ruined cairn that has just three stones of its retaining circle showing above the turf.

Top: The cist lying alongside the conifer plantation and (inset) the stones of the cist

Left: The view across cist No.1 and (above) the stones of the cist

South-west of Bellever Tor, near the crest of Black Hill, is a cist (No.1), all four stones of which survive more or less how they were originally placed. The internal dimensions of the cist are 5′ on one side and 5′ 6″ at the other; its width is 29″ at one end and 27″ at the other. No cap stone can be seen and very little of its cairn, however, four members of its retaining circle stand well clear of the turf, two on the north-east of the cist and two on the south-west. The lie of the cist is 61°NNW.

View across cist No.2 and (inset) the stones of the cist

Cist No.2 lies on the summit of Black Hill, only two stones survive today, the rest no doubt robbed for the building of the nearby wall. To give some idea of the size of the cist, the side stone is 48" long, and the end stone 35". Very little remains of its cairn, however seven stones of varying size belonging to its retaining circle have survived to show well above the moorland turf. The lie of the cist is 61°NNW.

Cist No.3 lies to the south-south-east of the previously-mentioned monument, on the other side of the newtake wall. Now shrouded in long moorland grass, it can be located by walking along the disused leat for about seventy-five paces then turning right and take another forty paces to the site of the cist. All four stones remain in place. Its internal dimensions are 49" along one side stone and 46" along its opposite number. Its width is 16" at both ends. No cap stone can be seen, and very little of its cairn except for two of the retaining circle. The lie of the cist is 2°NNE.

View across cist No.3 and (right) the stones of the cist

To the south of Laughter Tor will be seen a beautiful salmon-pink coloured menhir (below). After being found prostrate on the moorland floor, it was re-erected in 1893. It stands just over eight and half feet high at the head of a double stone row.

Possible ruined cist and cap stone

Over the Newtake wall, to the south-east of cist No.2, close to the disused leat that runs around the hillside, can be found what is thought to be the ruins of a cist, only one large elongated stone of which displays itself beneath a huge growth of gorse. It measures 61" in length. Its lie is 62°NNW. If it is the side stone of a cist, the stone lying prostrate in the photograph above could well be a section of its cap stone.

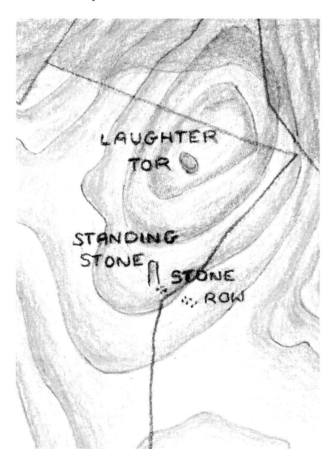

Laughter Tor double stone row

The Laughter Tor double stone row, is much depleted no doubt owing to the building of the newtake wall that runs through it. The row runs from near the crest of the hill to the south-east where its larger stones will be found, one standing at over four and half feet tall.

This monument known locally as the 'Money Pit' can be found high above Dartmeet, close to the left hand side of the road to Sherwell. Only one side stone and one end stone now remain of the cist. To give some idea of its size the side stone measures 36", the length of the end stone to where it meets the side stone is 16". The retaining circle still has eleven stones standing in place with a large empty space that could well have held two more. There are three stones in line that sit inside the outer ring. The cap stone lies to one side of the cist, the cist's lie is 63°NNW.

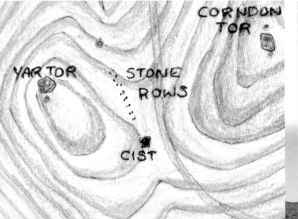

The view across the 'Money Pit' cist and (inset) the stones of the cist

The view over the triple stone row looking towards Sherwell

About 86 yards to the north of the last mentioned monument, a triple stone row, once more or less completely shrouded in gorse, can be located running down the hill towards the tiny hamlet of Sherwell. There is no evidence, no sign of any socket holes where stones may have once stood to suggest that the row once began its travel from the so-called 'Money Pit'. Most of the stones are of no great height, the tallest being no more than two feet high; however there are a few stones now lying prostrate that may have been a little higher, one with its socket hole still displaying a depth of about six inches. Until swaling took place in 2012 it would have been impossible to provide photographic evidence of it being a triple alignment due to the dense vegetation.

The monument has been served badly over the years with a reave being constructed across its path and gullies of some sort cut within the alignments to eventually undermine a few stones which now lie prostrate. Many of the stones are missing, most likely having been robbed for use in the construction of the lane that runs down to Sherwell, only a few yards away to its right. There is very little sign of the three rows within the last few yards of its run before its terminating cairn is met. This structure, shown in the photograph below, and now shrouded in heather, had its centre delved into many years ago.

Below: The terminating cairn of the triple stone row and (inset) after swaling, the stones of the triple stone row became more apparent

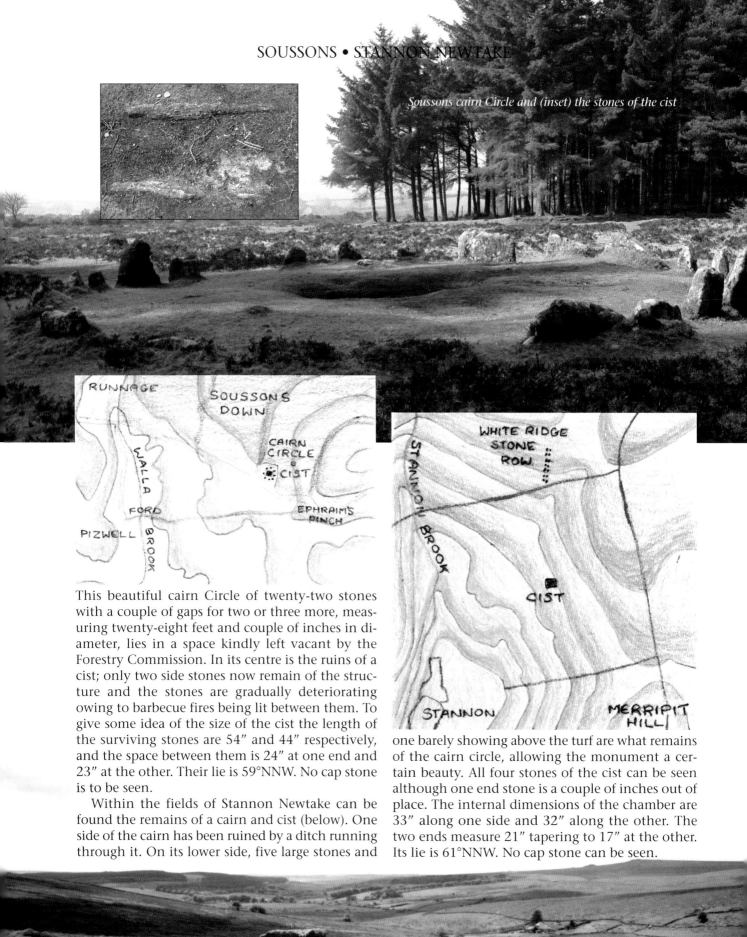

Soussons cairn Circle and (inset) the stones of the cist

This beautiful cairn Circle of twenty-two stones with a couple of gaps for two or three more, measuring twenty-eight feet and couple of inches in diameter, lies in a space kindly left vacant by the Forestry Commission. In its centre is the ruins of a cist; only two side stones now remain of the structure and the stones are gradually deteriorating owing to barbecue fires being lit between them. To give some idea of the size of the cist the length of the surviving stones are 54" and 44" respectively, and the space between them is 24" at one end and 23" at the other. Their lie is 59°NNW. No cap stone is to be seen.

Within the fields of Stannon Newtake can be found the remains of a cairn and cist (below). One side of the cairn has been ruined by a ditch running through it. On its lower side, five large stones and one barely showing above the turf are what remains of the cairn circle, allowing the monument a certain beauty. All four stones of the cist can be seen although one end stone is a couple of inches out of place. The internal dimensions of the chamber are 33" along one side and 32" along the other. The two ends measure 21" tapering to 17" at the other. Its lie is 61°NNW. No cap stone can be seen.

The Double stone row on White Ridge Hill

North of the previously-mentioned monument, on the far side of the newtake wall, a double stone row can be found. When I counted the stones that run down the southern slopes of White Ridge Hill, only twenty-five stones of the alignment now show above the turf and a great many of those that are merely an inch or so high are heavily shrouded by the tall moorland grass. No termination of the rows can be located at their lower end. The sad remains of their cairn, situated on the higher ground, is now recognisable only by a few heaps of stone rising a few inches above the surface of the moor.

Isolated high up on the moor above the beginnings of the Lade Hill Brook can be found the ruins of a cairn and cist. Nine stones, three standing, three leaning and three recumbent can be associated with the monument's inner cairn circle, while three stones of an outer circle can also be noticed outside the inner ring. There appears to be only one side stone that has survived the ruining of the cist which is 59" in length. The lie of this stone is 59°NNW.

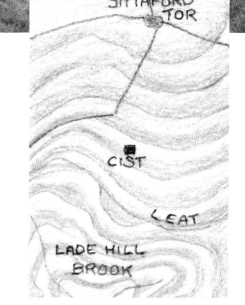

Lade Hill cairn and (inset) the stones of the cist

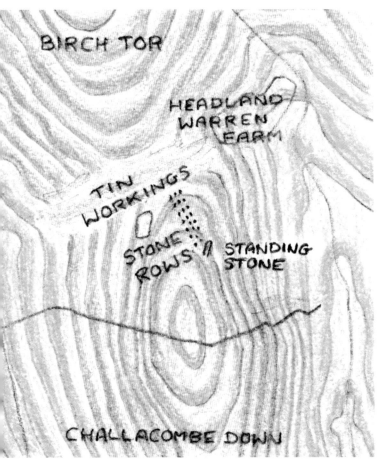

The Challacombe Down blocking stone

This triple stone row first recognised by Prideaux. runs down the northern slopes of Challacombe Down beginning with a blocking stone. At about eight and half feet in height, it is much taller than is usual. William Crossing tells us in his *Guide to Dartmoor* that it was first recorded in 1830. Samuel Rowe tells us that Rev. Baring-Gould considered there to be eight rows, three of which are perfect. Whether the rows ever had a cairn related to them at its northern end, only the excavators of the

Chaw Gully tin delvings would know, for it was these men who ripped the stones out of the earth that once held them upright. It is at the northern end of the alignments that we see the larger stones, but from here they diminish in size and become thinner on the ground as they travel up the incline towards the blocking stone. Baring-Gould's thinking, was that the set stones situated at the lower end and to the west of the alignments, were of five imperfect rows. Hansford Worth translates them as "presenting a stone circle, and some additional rows, very short and very imperfect", and supposed that the stones were part of the three Alignments that had been uprooted by the tinners and were then respectfully placed to one side of their workings. Give or take a few feet, the length of the alignments is about one hundred and seventy six yards from the first stone in the north to the blocking stone uphill to the South.

The Challacombe Down stone row

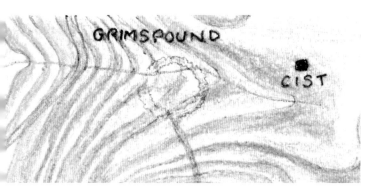

Grimspound. What can be said that hasn't been said before about this place? It is the most famous prehistoric site on Dartmoor, a site that even the less abled walker can enjoy. Its ramparts, although tumbled, can still be seen as most impressive. Two dozen hut circles, some erected for human habita-

tion with others perhaps for livestock, occupy the nigh on four-acre site. There is also a couple of features that appear to be courtyards attached to the walling at the lower end of the Pound; one almost beside the stream, 'Grims Lake', that runs through the site and probably supplied water for the original occupants. Four other courtyards are sited close to where most visitors enter the Pound. In 1894 Robert Burnard and the Rev. Baring-Gould, along with others, investigated twenty hut circles, revealing materials that in thirteen of them humans once resided. The others, it was concluded, must have been for storage or domestic animals. William Crossing had thought that the walls of the Pound was infilled with soil, whereas Baring-Gould tells us that if that was the case, all manner of plant life would now be growing from between the stones.

View over Grimspound
Middle: The entrance to Grimspound
Bottom: One of the hut circles within Grimspound

127

*The view across the Grims Lake cist
and (inset) the interior of the cist*

A few yards to the north of where the tiny Grims Lake stream seeps out of the earth, can be found a cist. All four stones of its chamber are still in place, with one side stone 35″ long, not quite touching one end stone. The internal length of its opposite number is 42″. The width of the cist is 24″ at one end, tapering slightly to 22″ at the other. Two cap stones that are employed to cover the cist, sit askew on top of it. Its lie is 52°WNW. The whole sits in the centre of its cairn circle of which ten stones survive today, with two that may have formed an outer circle.

On Shapley Common, on the western side of the road to Challacombe, just above the head of the East Bovey river, there are several hut circles. One in particular is a great example and can be seen clearly from the road as people pass by in their cars. It displays huge slabs of granite that forms its western wall while the stones of the hut's eastern wall have sadly fallen inward. This old dwelling, along with others, were examined by the Dartmoor Exploration Committee a year after they excavated the huts at Grimspound, but found nothing of any significance. For this feature only, I have moved away from the watershed theme for the purpose of showing one of the best examples of a hut circle on the moor.

Shapley Common hut circle

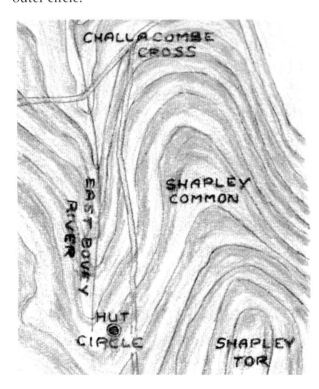

Hamel Down cairn and (inset) the stones of the cist

At the southern end of Hamel Down just to the left of the Two Moors Way track as one descends the hill, lies this ruined cist (above). One end stone still sits in place, while the existence of the other, without excavation, is uncertain. However both sides are there to be seen with one of them comprising two slabs. Its width can be determined at 32" at one end tappering slightly to 30" at the other. Its lie, surprisingly varies at 38° to 40°SW. The cist must have had two stones to cap it, for one is still in place covering just part. It sits in the ruins of its cairn which displays just a couple stones of its retaining circle.

This cist (below) is on the saddle of Blackslade Down, to the right of the track before it drops downhill towards Tunhill. Its internal measurements are 42" and 40" along the sides respectively; width-wise it is 30" tappering to 27". Its lie is North. There is a slab of granite lying to one side of the cist that could well be one section of its cap stone. Little of its cairn now exists.

Blackslade cairn ruins and (inset) the stones of the cist

CUT HILL

High up above the infant waters of the East Dart river, on Cut Hill, can be found the exposed granite slabs of a Neolithic stone row. Archaeologist Dr Tom Greeves apparently was the first to mention its existence in 2004. The nine stones all lying prostrate run in a line at more or less ESE–WNW. It is not yet known for sure as to whether the row had ever been standing.

I investigated those stones that display their full lengths and that follow one another in a line. To give some idea of the distances between the stones, (all measurement being approximate) from No.1 to No.2 it is 83'; between stones 2 and 3 it is 88'; between stones 3 and 4 it is 55'; between stones 4 and 5 it is 60'; between stone 5 and 6 there is a peat hag about 4' in height (which may contain a seventh stone); from stone 5 to the SE edge of the hag is 20'. The width of the hag is 53ft and from the NW edge of the hag to stone No.6 is 12' 6".

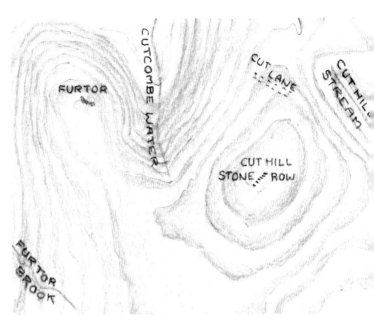

Stone No.1 – 7' 4" long

Stone No.2 – 7' 10" long

Stone No.3 – 6' 4" long

Stone No.4 – 6' 8" long

Stone No.5 – 8' 10" long

Stone No.6 – 6' 9" long

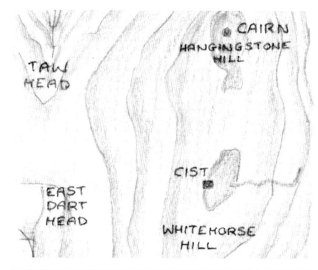

*Excavating the cist and
(inset above) the stones of
the exposed cist*

From the Cut Hill monument we now cross into the River Teign watershed, to Whitehorse Hill, to a peat hag (not much bigger than the average lock-up garage). Here in the year 2000, Jim Turner came across a cist buried in the peat. What was thought to be the end stone had fallen out exposing the interior of the monument, including the base stone, an unusual feature among Dartmoor cists. What was thought to be the end stone was in fact a side stone that it had slipped outwards, the peat being eroded due to the rigours of the high moorland climate. At this height of 1,973 feet, it is the loftiest situated known cist on Dartmoor.

To prevent further erosion, a drystone wall was erected alongside the little monument, the stones of which can now be seen lying on the ground. All of them were removed to expose the cist for the work of archaeologists to begin.

It took three days of painstaking intricate toil to expose every related stone, so as to allow for their carefully-measured removal. However, to the astonishment of those working on it, there was an extra surprise, for there on the base stone, after examination, were found shale beads and beads made from amber. There was also a piece of animal hide 'thought to be that of a wolf', but not verified, and there was a specimen of a plant, small strips of leather, that had been worked, and what appeared to be a woven bag, with its stitching still in place, along with cremated bone and charcoal.

On the outside of the cist two wooden stakes were found,

believed to be of hazel, sharpened to a point, one lying in an horizontal position, the other standing beside one of the end stones. The base stone was later taken to a laboratory for closer examination.

The photo above shows the space in the peat hag after the cist was removed. The photo below left displays the stones that made up the cist, minus the base stone, each with a label tied firmly around it for identification purposes, the cover stone, that can be seen on the left measures thirty-one and half inches by twenty three and five- eighths of an inch.

The photo below right shows the cist back in place and partially buried; it also reveals that two stones did indeed make up the exposed side that had fallen out on to the ground. No cairn seems to have been associated with this cist.

The photographs of the excavation included here were kindly provided by the Dartmoor National Park Archaeological Department (copyright reserved). I also thank them for the archaeological information concerning the exciting finds associated with the cist.

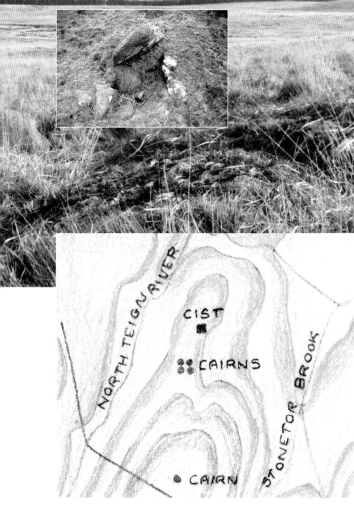

Above: View over the Stonetor Brook cairn and (inset) the stones of the cist

Grey Wethers stone circles, lie down hill to the east of Sittaford Tor, situated on a saddle between the Dart watershed and that of the Teign. However the rainwater that falls on this site eventually runs into the latter. The southern circle is slightly larger in diameter than its northern counterpart by roughly 5 feet. It is in fact the largest of the eleven stone circles on the whole of Dartmoor. When William Crossing first examined them in 1878, he counted 27 stones in the southern circle with only 7 standing, where as in the northern circle only 16 stones could be ascertained, with 9 standing.

To be found on a ridge, between the North Teign river and the Stonetor Brook are the sad remains of a cist. Before the ruin is reached from the south, the walker will pass five cairns. All the stones of the cist, with one side being made up of two stones, still survive, albeit a little roughed up, along with the cap stone that has been pushed to one side. However, all are still enclosed within its cairn. The cist can be said to be more or less square in section with a rough measurement of 32″ by 32″. Its lie is 54°NWW.

*　　*　　*

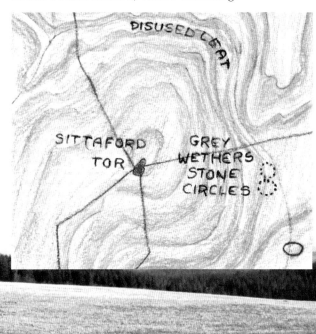

John L.W. Page who produced the sketch of the Grey Wethers circles (see left), for the engraver Alfred Dawson to portray, recorded the same numbers. The newtake wall could well be the culprit for the sad state of the circles, each was thought by G.W. Ormerod to have originally contained thirty-two of these relatively slim slabs of granite. Samuel Rowe when he saw them, suggested that the stones had been worked so as to form square heads, as did Burnard. Yet if one looks at some of the natural stone slabs on Sittaford Tor (like the one in the photo below), from where the stones of the circles were no doubt brought, they have a characteristic square edge. During early excavations, ash was found beneath the turf suggesting to some that the circles were used for cremations or even sacrifices. Both were underwent restoration in 1909 under the guidance of Robert Burnard.

This photo and above: The Grey Wethers stone circles and (inset) natural granite slabs on Sittaford Tor.

Assycombe Double stone row

The Assycombe Hill double stone row lies in the vast acreage of Fernworthy Forest. It is best approached from the southern end, following a track through the forest for a short half a mile. The monument will be seen on the left running down the hill from a cairn to its blocking stone at the bottom. The cairn still holds in its fold a side stone of a cist 51" in length, shown in the photo below. 15 stones can still be counted circling the cairn. Leading the row down the hill is a menhir 6' 8" in height standing at right angles to the rows; another stone, fallen, is 6' 9" in length. All the stones along the row's length are short with the tallest being no more than 18" high. The black and white photo was taken by Robert Burnard, during the later part of the 1890s.

Left: Assycombe double stone row, looking up the row from the blocking stone.

Right: Side stone of the cist.

Below: Assycombe Double stone row as photographed by Robert Burnard in May 1894.

135

Hurston double stone row

Hurston double stone row blocking stone

Out on the open moor, on the gentle slopes of Hurston Ridge which commands the most spectacular views, can be seen another double stone row. This alignment however, unlike that at Assycombe, has no stones missing from its fifty pairs. As with the Assycombe rows the stones run downhill from a cairn. This cairn is almost non existent; laid just about flat, and spread about, possibly by those searching for the treasure which they thought might be buried within.

As with the rows of their neighbour down in the forest, the alignments here have a standing stone at their outset. Measuring 5' 10" in height this stone stands in line with the stones of the eastern row. Again, like the Assycombe alignments, a blocking stone, 3' 10" high, concludes the extent of the western row. It is surprising that during R.H. Worth's comprehensive survey of the monument, he did not mention the fallen enclosure wall that intersects the alignments about a third of the way along its travel. Which came first, perhaps only an excavation of the site can tell us.

Hurston double stone row

FERNWORTHY RESERVOIR

Down beside Fernworthy Reservoir lies a cist in superb condition with its cap stone leaning to one side of it, propped up on two stone that balance on one side stone. The height of the construction of the dam wall helped to save this grave from ending up below water level and away from our view altogether except during the times of drought. Both side stones and end stones are still in their original positions; the internal measurements of the sides are 42″ and 39″ respectively, while the width at one end is 22″ and 21″ at the other. Is lie is 55°WNW.

Within confines of the cairn, that has been delved into quite considerably, there was another cist (shown in the bottom photo on this page). It was taken to and exhibited for some years at the Torquay museum. It now lies in the garden of the Princetown offices of Dartmoor National Park. Like the cist that still lies beside the water at Fernworthy, it is intact with its cap leaning on one of the side stones. Its internal dimensions are 43″ along one side and 42″ on the other; its width is 20″ at one end and 22″ at the other.

Back in the forest again can be found a prehistoric complex that is as interesting as any on the Dartmoor. Now, but for the stone circle (above), the complex is quite dilapidated. There are three stone rows, two double and one single. Although ruinous there are three cairns associated with a row and two that are isolated. Ensconced in the remains of the cairn that heads the single row is a side stone and end stone of a cist (above right). To give some idea of the size of the cist the one end stone is 27", while the side stone is 31".

The row that runs away from this cairn and cist is so overgrown and depleted in its numbers that a photograph is impossible to obtain, but a row that can be photographed is found just yards away through a gap in the trees (below). However, the stones are small and just a couple stand no more than twelve inches above the turf, with most barely pushing their heads above the ground.

In order to count them one had to be quite diligent, using feet as well as eyes and hands. For there are 29 stones along the two lines, 18 pairs 11 singles. But it was back in 1979 when I counted them; the last time I walked between the rows they were overgrown.

138

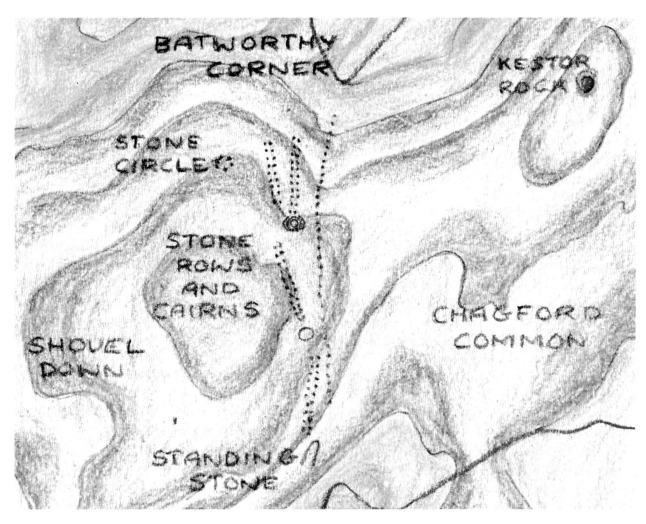

Out on Shovel Down on the open moor, to the north-north-east of the last described alignments, can be found perhaps the most comprehensive prehistoric complex on the moor. This includes the ruins of five more rows, the remains of a stone circle, a menhir and a fourfold cairn circle. Four of the rows are definitely double in their design. All the rows have been robbed of several of their members for use elsewhere. Sadly only three members of the stone circle now stand in place, two of which are shown below. Although R.H. Worth made a comprehensive survey of the Shovel Down complex he did not mention the ruined circle which can be found uphill WNW of stone row No.3.

*Two of the three remaining stones
in the stone circle*

139

SHOVEL DOWN

Row No.1, running more or less to the north, can be followed uphill from a menhir standing ten and half feet in height (the Long Stone as it is known on Dartmoor), to where it ends today with quite a disappointing pair of stones. All the stones in the row are no more than twelve inches high with some barely showing above the turf, though several could well be hidden beneath the long tough growth of moorland grass that shrouds several yards of the row. Its length, taken in 2013, was 488' 9". Only 29 stones can be seen, 18 of which still stand in their original pairs.

Right: Shovel Down Long Stone.

Top: The last of the stones in Row 1.

Above: The same stones looking south.

Stone row No.2 starts with what remains of a cairn, approximately 105 feet to the north of the end stones of row No.1. This monument is longer at 658', and runs to the north-west. All the stones are substantial in size with the tallest being 36" in height. There are 71 stones to be counted, of which there are twenty-two pairs still standing; beyond the last pair there is a gap of about one hundred and six feet to the last stone to be seen upright. This specimen stands by itself. Altogether there are ten stones that are prostrate, three of which can be found in the considerable empty space, now isolated from the rest. The photograph above is looking down the row from the cairn, while the photograph below is looking up the row. Inset: the last stone of the row.

The scant remains of row No.3 lie almost unnoticed to the east of row No.2. It is 623' long from where it appears to begin in the south, to where its last stones can be seen in the north. No cairn or blocking stone is to be found at either end of this sad spectacle of a row. There are 48 member stones to be counted, some of which cannot be seen but can be felt below the thick moorland grass. There are only twelve pairs that remain standing. The photograph above shows the row's beginning. Below, the photo on the left shows the stones at the northern end of the row while the photograph opposite it displays the middle section of the row. Its direction lies to the north-west.

Row No.4 is perhaps the most photogenic of the five alignments. It begins it travel from a fourfold cairn circle. Ahead of this can be seen a fallen menhir now, like the Long Stone, employed as a parish boundary mark, in this instance 'GP' – Gidleigh Parish. In front of the menhir is another fallen stone fronting an impressive double row of stones until they peter out into gaps of several feet until the last two are met. The whole, from the centre of the fourfold cairn circle, is 602' long. There are eleven doubles still in place. The whole runs to the north. The photograph below shows the fallen menhirs, the longest being (inset) the 'GP'-etched boundary stone in front of the circle.

Above: Row 4 doubles that remain standing, plus the two that have fallen and (below) the last two stones that remain standing of Row 4

Stone row No.5 is described by the author of *Worth's Dartmoor* as running more or less to the NNW where it overlaps row No.1; but today no stones can be found. There is another plan of this row in Jeremy Butler's series *Dartmoor Atlas of Antiquities*, again showing the row veering to the NNW before approaching the cairn of row No.2. It then veers gradually to the north and comes to a halt before reaching the stone walling of Batworthy Corner. Very little can be found of this monument, the stones either hidden beneath the thick moorland grass or they have been robbed for work elsewhere. There is one seemingly set stone at the top of the hill, lying approximately fifteen paces to the east of row No.1; it stands 22″ high and aligns 2°N. The next stone that can be found that could belong to the alignment stands erect beside a track that runs uphill from Batworthy Corner, again this aligns 2°N. It stands erect at about 20″ high.

Back in the nineteenth century, the antiquarian John L. W. Page had the idea that in all probability, the Shovel Down stone rows did at one time connect with the complex down at Fernworthy, as well as the next feature to be viewed, that is of the beautiful Scorhill stone circle. Page's plan of the site is shown below.

Top: A set stone, possible remnant of row No.5

Above: Possible remnant of row No.5 beside the Batworthy track

Right: John Page's plan of the Shovel Down rows

Scorhill stone circle, across the river Teign from Shovel Down, is one of the most accessible on the moor. Over the years it has been robbed of several of its members, with 23 still standing in situ, the loftiest being 7' 5" high. Lying prostrate on the turf near the southern portions of the monument, can be seen three of its original members. One with an end cut off (below left), measures 5' 10". Two that display the holes of the feather and tare (below centre and right), measure 6' 6", and 7' 3"; they were no doubt destined to be taken away to be employed as gateposts. It is generally thought that four stones that once formed part of the circle's majestic appearance, now secure the right bank of the Scorhill leat (above right), that can be seen running along the hillside, just a few yards away.

About two-thirds of a mile to the north-west of Scorhill Circle will be found the sad remains of another circle on the slopes of Buttern Hill (above). There are fourteen stones, although only five remain standing, the tallest being just under 24". Several are leaning, like the two in the photograph below; others are no doubt buried. The longest fallen stone is 6' 11" which, when standing, could well have been the monument's tallest.

On the lower eastern slopes of Buttern Hill, a few yards from the lower edge of a walled field, can be found among the gorse the ruins of a chambered cairn, one of just a few to be found on Dartmoor. However, this specimen is the best there is. It is 10' 6" long, and 42" at its widest inner measurement. What appears to be the monument's entrance, facing to the east, is 20" wide. On the floor in front of this feature lies a large flat elongated slab forming a step up to entrance. All sits on a slight mound. The cairn's lie is 6°NNE.

Top: Remains of Buttern Hill stone circle . Above left: Leaning stones from the remains of the circle. Above right: Ruins of a chambered cairn

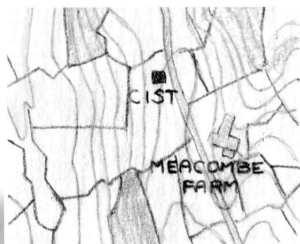

Out off the moor in the fields of the in-country, can be located the so called Meacombe burial chamber. Permission must be sought to visit this site, for it is on private land. The internal length of the chamber is 3' 5", its width is 19". Its height to the top of its cap stone is 4' 1'. According to R.H. Worth, this solid block of granite weighs over two tons and in *Worth's Dartmoor* he tells us that both of the end stones of this feature were stolen. The internal measurements of the chamber is, but for a couple inches, more or less the same as most Dartmoor cists. Its lie is 54°WNW. The photograph above displays the end view of the Chamber, the one below is a view of the side, where one can see where the end stones may have once been placed.

A mile or so to the north-east of Mortonhampstead lies Mardon Down, where can be found the dilapidated ruin of a stone circle. Photographs of the north (left) and south (above) sections are shown. It is 124' in diameter, the largest circle to be found in the National Park, and twenty-one member stones of various shapes and sizes can be counted, but only six of them now remain standing. The largest of these shown in the photo on the left, measures 4' 2" high by 8' 8" long. There are seven cairns of various shapes and sizes and in various conditions of preservation to be seen. which includes the so called 'Giants Grave'. On the other side of the hill, to the left of the track, sitting amongst the gorse is a small cairn which has been seriously delved into. A few yards further on, overlooking the in-country to the north, will be found the intriguing remains of the cairn circle, pictured below. This interesting monument appears to include a kerb of stones lying horizontally around the outside of a inner Circle of upright stones.

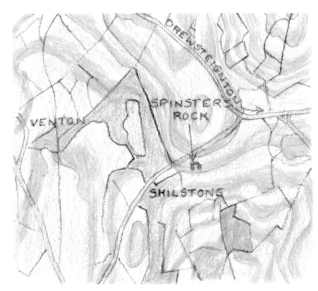

Spinsters Rock, the only surviving recognised dolmen in the Dartmoor National Park, and this is a restoration. It was restored in 1862 the same year that it collapsed to the ground. In the centre of the monument its height from floor to cap stone is six feet, all but a half an inch. The cap stone itself, is at its thickest, approximately 36", it's length is 14' 9", and its width is 9' 7". It has been estimated that it weighs around 16 tons. There is an old wives' tales associated with the monument, about how three spinsters erected it one morning before they sat down for their breakfast. The structure is in fact a burial chamber of the Neolithic period. The nineteenth century antiquarian Polwhele in his writings, tells us that there were in his time, other prehistoric remains associated with this dolmen, two stone rows in fact and several stone circles. The Rev. Gray, in 1838 with his brother visited the dolmen and its surroundings and searched for the remains referred to by Polwhele and discovered them to the north of the monument. Gray tells us that he found and mapped the stone avenues and concentric stone circles. However, when G.W. Ormerod visited the site in 1862, these were all gone, no doubt robbed for the building of stone walls and dwellings nearby to the north.

*Houndtor cairn and cist and
(inset) the remains of the cist*

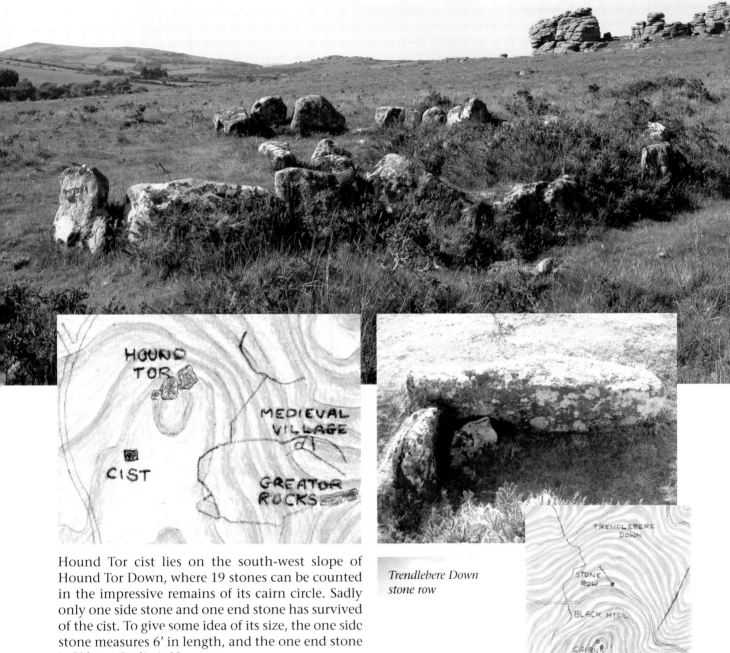

*Trendlebere Down
stone row*

Hound Tor cist lies on the south-west slope of Hound Tor Down, where 19 stones can be counted in the impressive remains of its cairn circle. Sadly only one side stone and one end stone has survived of the cist. To give some idea of its size, the one side stone measures 6' in length, and the one end stone is 2' long. Its lie is N.

Trendlebere Down stone row, now shrouded in gorse and heather, can be found on the lower slopes of Black Hill, just a little over thirty yards north of the Haytor–Manaton road. There is a twin pair os stones near its northern end that suggests that this monument was at one time, a double row, now much robbed. It begins its travel from a much ruined cairn. The last time I viewed the site only nineteen stones could be counted. None are of any great height, the tallest being no more than three feet high, and not all are standing, the length of the longest being 4' 6". The length of the row to the last stone is approximately 394'.

COSDON HILL

Cosdon Hill triple stone row

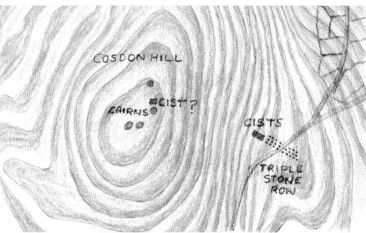

Cosdon Hill lower cist

Cosdon Hill higher cist

Up on the eastern side of Cosdon Hill, where the gradient isn't so fierce, lies a triple stone row approximately 447' long from the centre of the cairn to the last remaining stone. Sadly the alignment has been cut through by the South Zeal peat track which leaves a great scar across the face of this beautiful monument. The rows begin their travel with their initial outset stones set at right angles to the alignment's run, and intriguingly are deliberately offset, with one leading off before the others.

In the fold of the cairn lies the remains of two cists. To give some idea of the size of these graves, the chamber nearest the row, and still displaying its cap stone, measures 51" by 33". The cist next to it, has only one side stone remaining, measuring 47" while sharing the 33" end stone of its neighbour. Both cists have a lie of 57°NW, while the rows themselves run more or less to the east.

152

COSDON BEACON

Way above the last described remains is Cosdon Beacon, really a huge cairn that William Crossing described as being ninety yards in diameter. One must apply some imagination to picture the folk of yesteryear setting light to a huge pile of timber to warn of any danger that might be on its way.

Here can be found four sites of interest. Just around 82' from the huge cairn can be found a Ring cairn 66' in diameter. Another, but smaller ring cairn, 52' in diameter, can be found further to the north. This feature has an outer kerb of stones and at one time, according to Samuel Rowe, accommodated a cist in its midst; perhaps the few stones in a heap are all that remain. Still further to the north will be found the smallest of the monuments, it being the usual type of cairn. Here in the centre of its pile will be seen the ruins of a cist shown in the photo below left. Its length can be more or less ascertained at 44" and its width at 29". Its lie is 59°NNW. Further on to the north a much larger cairn (pictured lower right), still displays a considerable portion of its stone circle.

LITTLE HOUND TOR

Little Hound Tor stone circle.

White Moor Menhir.

Just over a mile to the south of the last mentioned complex, can be found the Little Hound Tor stone circle. Sixteen stones can be seen standing, the tallest being just over 45". Two have fallen, one on the north-west side and one on the south-east side are missing. In William Crossing's day only thirteen stood erect, and only one was standing in 1897 when the Dartmoor Exploration Committee undertook the task of erecting the fallen stones again. Not far off to the south-east can be seen the so called White Moor Stone, a boundary marker of the 1240 Perambulation of the Forest of Dartmoor. Along with other inscribed marks on the stone, the Duchy 'DC' can be seen quite clearly near the top of the menhir. According to Crossing, the stone stands at about 5' 6" high. It has been suggested that the stone was dragged to this spot from the stone circle; perhaps this is possibility, it could well be one of the missing stones of the circle. If it was manhandled from the circle, it would have been the tallest of that venerable monument by a clear 1' 9".

Could the feature in the photo above be the dilapidated cist William Crossing scantily describes as being found among the enclosures and hut circles on the hill above the Small Brook. The two stones measure 50″ and 33″ respectively. The lie of the longest stone is 58°NNW which corresponds with a great many of the cists on the moor.

The great recumbent stone in the photo below might well be the menhir Crossing also described; it has a measurement of 21′ 8″.

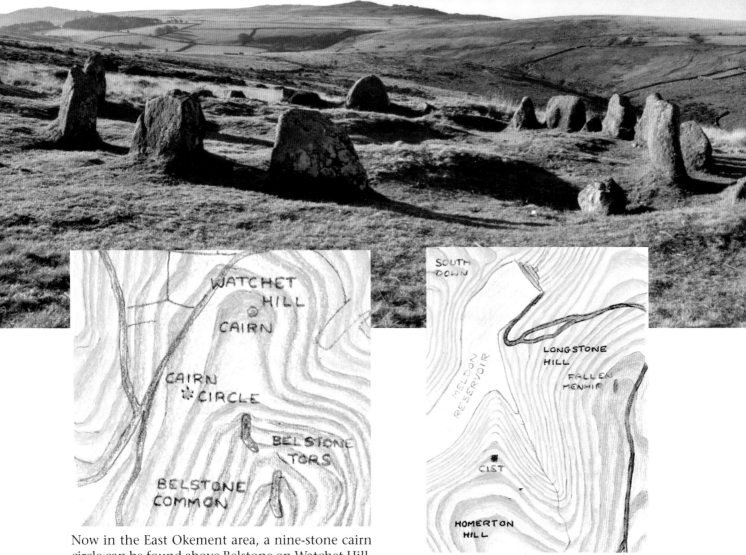

Belstone cairn Circle.

Now in the East Okement area, a nine-stone cairn circle can be found above Belstone on Watchet Hill. The monument actually has 16 stones in its circumference while there is one stone almost buried beneath the turf and several missing. If we look at the north-west side of the circle, there is hardly a space between the stones, and if this indicates the original design it can be estimated that to fill the gaps where stones appear to be missing, it could well take up to another 14 members. The centre has been crudely dug into and thrown to one side by the inquisitive or perhaps grave robbers.

On Longstone Hill there is a fallen and partially buried menhir 8' 11" long. At its widest point it is 37", and about halfway along its length it is 15" thick. Knowing this hill is more or less stone free, there is no doubt in my mind that this monolith was brought here from elsewhere to be purposefully erected on this spot. This hill no doubt took its name from the now recumbent stone that at one time stood erect here. Sharing this hill with the menhir, is a cemetery of two dozen cairns of all sizes and states of preservation.

HOMERTON HILL

Of the half dozen or so cairns on Homerton Hill, the cairn in the photograph above is the only one that contains a cist. To give some idea of its size (see below left), the side stones measure 49" and 48" respectively; the end stone at just 18", giving the grave a comparatively narrow dimension. Its lie is 4°NNE. A flat slab lying on the north side of the cairn could well be the cist's cap stone (below).

*　　　*　　　*

157

INDEX

This index of sites and monuments is arranged by the principal Dartmoor river valleys in the order in which they appear in the book. The reader will be able to identify the page on which individual sites and monuments can be found within each of these areas.